LIMOGES ENAMEL TRIPTYCHS

Museo Nazionale del Bargello

LIMOGES ENAMEL TRIPTYCHS

Three Masterpieces from the Carrand Collection

Edited by
Ilaria Ciseri and Riccardo Gennaioli

With an essay and catalogue entries by
Paola Venturelli

OFFICINA LIBRARIA

Art direction
Paola Gallerani

Design
Elisabetta Mancini

Translation
Sarah Elizabeth Cree

Editing
Wendy Keebler

Index of names
Marcella Culatti

Colour separation
Premani srl, Pantigliate (Milano)

Printed by
Petruzzi, Città di Castello (Perugia)

ISBN: 978-88-3367-196-3

Printed in Italy

Officina Libraria
Via dei Villini 10
00161 Roma

To keep up to date on catalogue titles, news, events, press reviews and additional content, visit:

officinalibraria.net
Officina.Libraria
officinalibraria

Acknowledgments
Elena Berardi
Benedetta Cantini
Marco Ciatti
Vincenzo De Magistris
Filippo Fornai
Marco Magni
Mattia Mercante
Andrea Nieddu
Paolo Parmiggiani
Sandra Rossi
Nicholas J. Stamm
Alexandra Toscano
Maria Cristina Valenti
Marco Verità
Dimitrios Zikos
Katherine Zock

Friends of the Bargello

Opificio delle Pietre Dure

TABLE OF CONTENTS

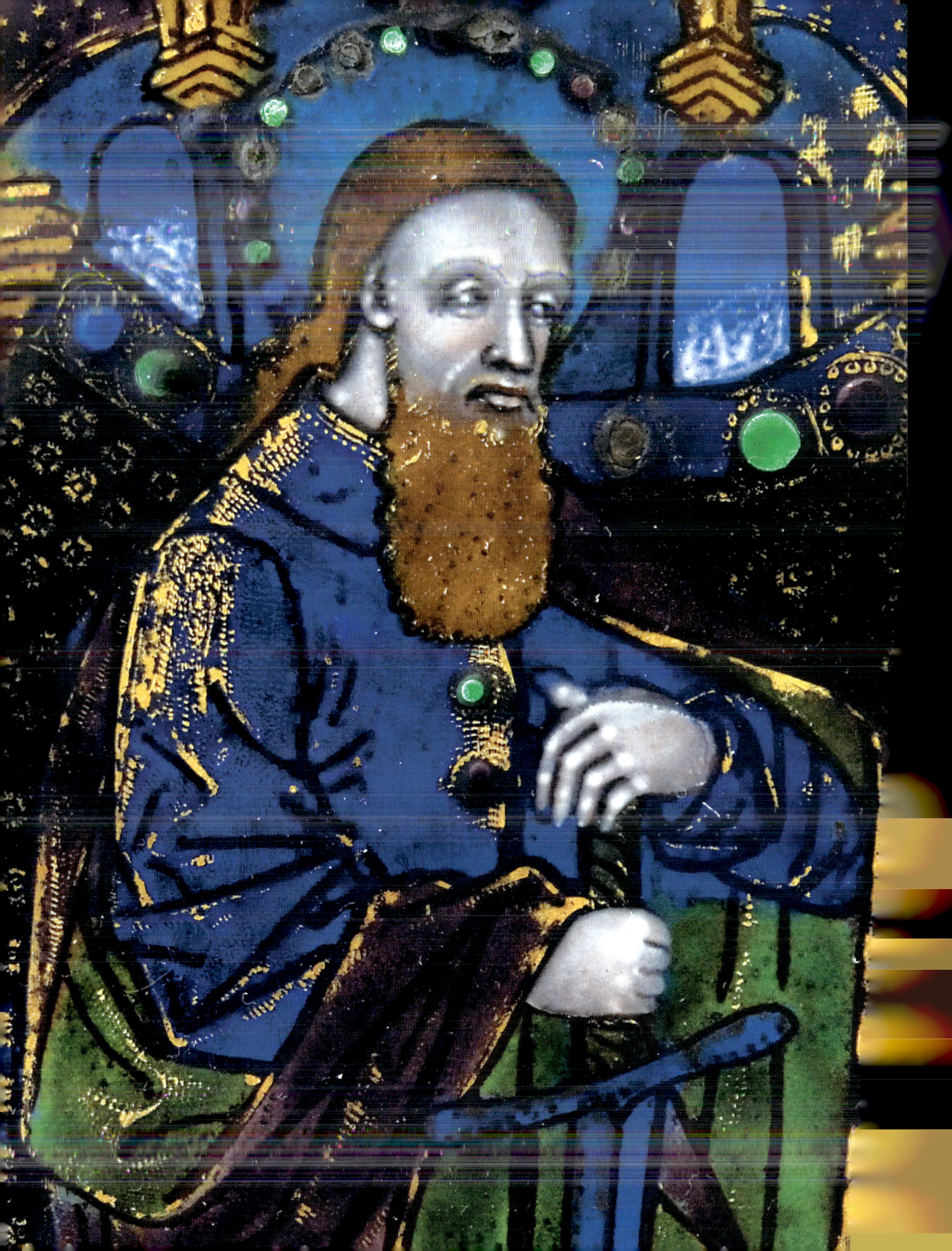

FOREWORD

The Louis Carrand collection, bequeathed to the Museo Nazionale del Bargello in 1888, enriched the museum with more than 2,500 works from different cultures and made using different techniques, from refined ivories to rare enamels, a full 140.
This important bequest changed the nature of the Bargello, making it one of the most important decorative art museums in Italy. The gallery known at the time as the Sala del Duca d'Atene was renamed after Louis Carrand and most of the works were put on view, including the enamels. A few changes were made later on and the current display dates to the 1980s.
The delicate nature of the enamels posed conservation problems over time linked to their display. For more than a decade, the Opificio delle Pietre Dure has been monitoring some of the Bargello's enamels and, in 2018, began the diagnostic analysis and restoration of the three triptychs, spearheaded by Ilaria Ciseri.
In 2021, it became essential to ensure the proper conversation and display of the three masterpieces. At a time of difficulty caused by the continuation of the pandemic, the support of Carolina Bucci and the Friends of the Bargello made it possible to create a new display case in the Carrand gallery.
This volume illustrates the exceptional quality of the enamels, returned to their full splendour and studied from different points of view. Ilaria Ciseri traces back over the role of Louis Carrand and his father Jean-Baptiste in the nineteenth-century rediscovery of enamels. Paola Venturelli examines enamel production in France in the early sixteenth century and artistic relationships with Italy and, in individual catalogue entries, takes an in-depth look at each of the triptychs.
Lastly, our colleagues at the Opificio meticulously explain the delicate work of restoring the enamels and the diagnostic analyses carried out.
I would like to thank Ilaria Ciseri for having overseen all the phases of this delicate project, emphasising its importance with Carolina Bucci and the Friends of the Bargello and then planning the production of this volume.
I would also like to thank Riccardo Gennaioli and our colleagues at the Opificio delle Pietre Dure, who carried out an exemplary restoration of works as valuable as they are fragile.
My profound gratitude goes to Carolina Bucci and the Friends of the Bargello who funded the creation of a new display case during an especially challenging year for the Musei del Bargello. My hope is that this will be the beginning of a new phase of scientific and museological attention to the wondrous and encyclopaedic Carrand collection.

PAOLA D'AGOSTINO
Director
Musei del Bargello

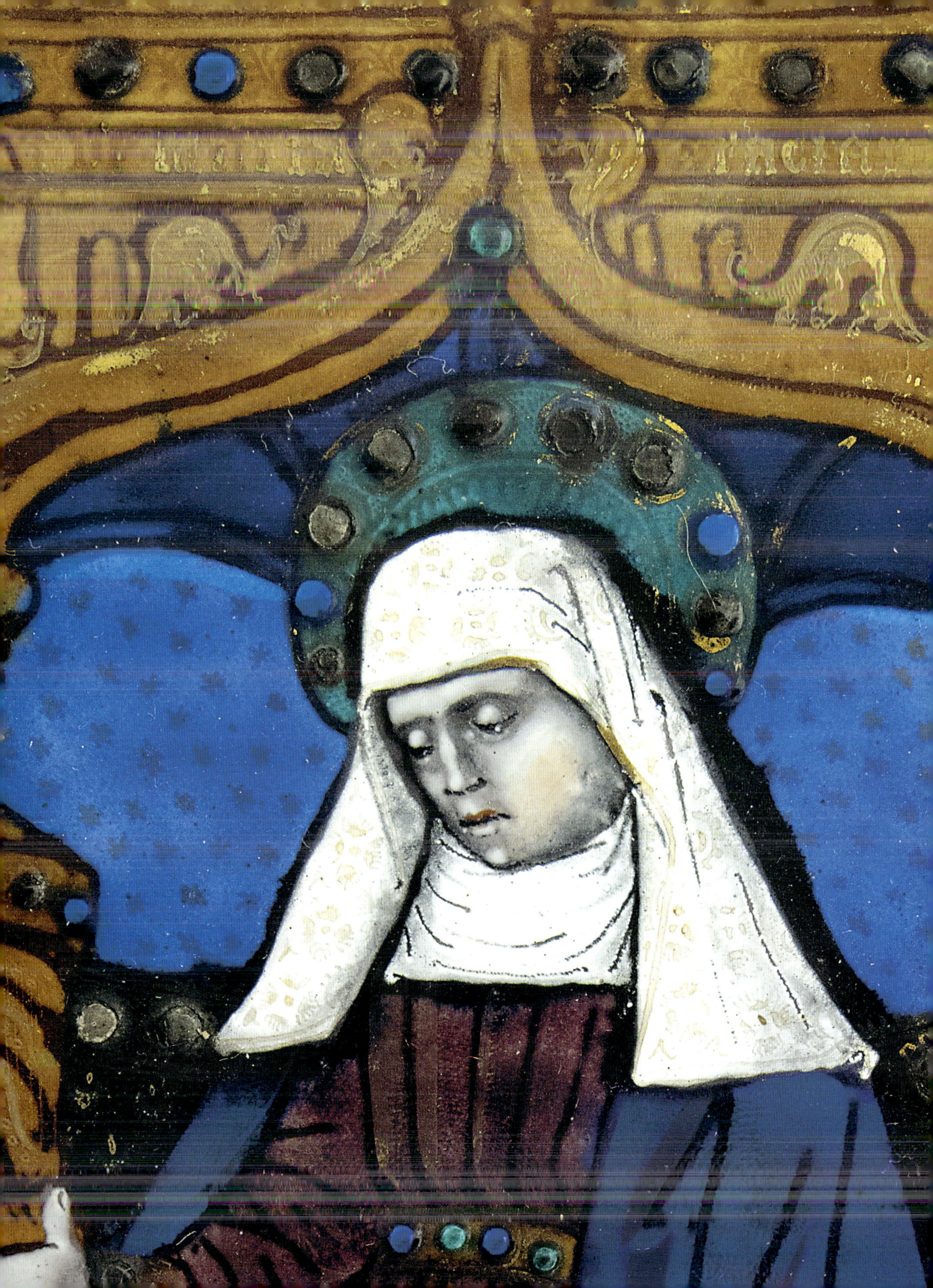

THE FRIENDS OF THE BARGELLO: A COMMITMENT TO CONSERVE AND PROMOTE THE CARRAND COLLECTION

One of the more rewarding positions for a charity is watching the chain of positivity that is triggered by its efforts. Too often daily mechanics obstruct the longer view, and our vision is obscured by layers of detail and focus on vital minutiae. Then suddenly, a project is completed like this one around these precious Limoges enamel triptychs, and we can see clearly the positivity that the Friends of the Bargello are increasingly able to offer this world-class museum, the Museo Nazionale del Bargello.

This project was a fascinating one, as it encompassed so many parts: critical conservation, research, publication, and reinstallation. Each part was contingent on the next, and together with the museum curator, Ilaria Ciseri, the Friends of the Bargello were able to direct the commitment of Carolina Bucci and James Pyner toward the significance of this project. It was through their generosity that the appropriate, specified display case could be purchased for these newly conserved, rarefied and historically important enamels.

This focused catalogue is a fine addition to the surprisingly limited research on late 15th and early 16th century Limoges painted enamel; a period of splendid production but one characterised by problematic, often conflicting opinions. Through the lens of these three masterpieces of enamel from the Carrand collection, clarity is introduced to this subject, and the significance of these enamelled triptychs is finally appreciated.

The Carrand collection of applied arts encompasses over 2,500 works of art and remains the most important collection of its type in Italy. Despite its importance, there are areas of this vast collection that have never been catalogued, properly researched, or published. The Friends of the Bargello are committed to supporting the Carrand collection in each of these areas of deserving need and look forward to our involvement in the next project dedicated to this great collection, a glorious repository of fine 19th century collector's taste and connoisseurship.

KATHERINE ZOCK
Vice President & Director
of The Friends of the Bargello

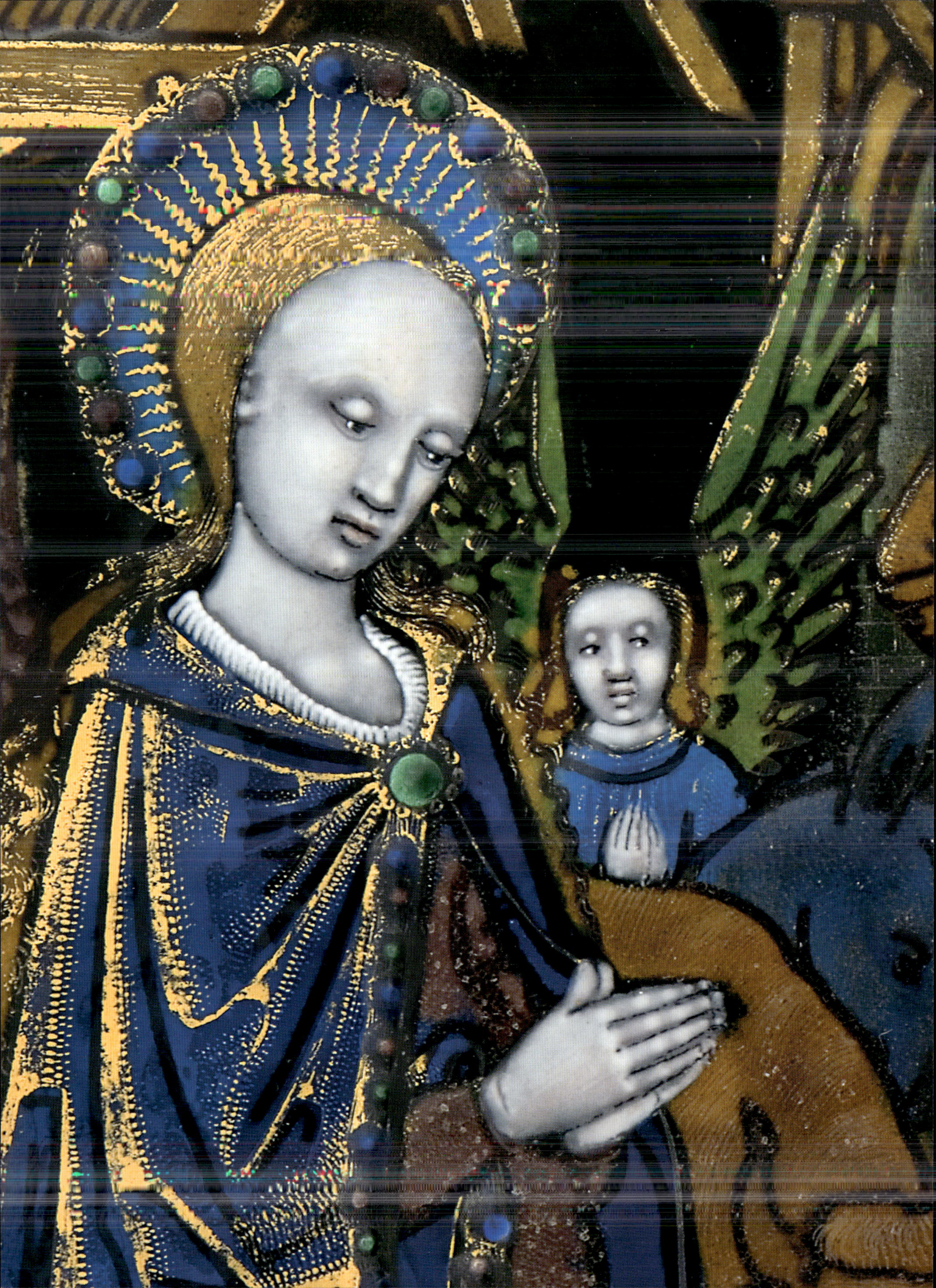

THREE ENAMEL MASTERPIECES FROM THE JEAN-BAPTISTE AND LOUIS CARRAND COLLECTION: A CASE OF DOCUMENTED FAME

When Léon de Laborde published the *Notice des émaux exposés dans les galeries du Musée du Louvre* in 1852, the Jean-Baptiste Carrand collection of enamels already included pieces important enough to be described in the text. The fact that the *Notice* included two of the three works to which this volume is dedicated is truly an extraordinary coincidence.

Three beautiful Renaissance triptychs in enamel on copper (*Man of Sorrows with the Virgin Mary and Saint John the Evangelist, Flanked by Saints Paul and Peter*, no. 1187 C; *Noli me tangere, Flanked by Myrrh Bearers*, no. 1188 C; *Adoration, Flanked by the Virgin Annunciate and the Archangel Gabriel*, no. 1189 C), which came to the Museo Nazionale del Bargello in 1888 with the Carrand collection, are now on display in a special new setting. Exquisite and gleaming but extremely fragile, these works presented enormous risks in terms of conservation, which were remedied by the timely intervention of the Settore Oreficerie (Goldsmithery Conservation Department) of the Opificio delle Pietre Dure (an art restoration institute of the Italian Ministry for Cultural Heritage).[1] To exhibit them, it was essential to first remove their wooden and fabric mounts (figs. 1–3), the cause of fatal chemical reactions in enamel, and, above all, to house them in a modern climate-controlled glass display case. Otherwise a challenging stretch for the museum budget, the latter has been gifted to the Bargello; thanks to the immense and timely generosity of Carolina Bucci, jewellery designer and creator of an internationally renowned brand, the museum has been able to purchase a Goppion display case of the highest quality, where the triptychs can finally enjoy an ideal microclimate.[2]

For the occasion, we are attempting to briefly retrace the historical journey these three enamels have taken to reach us today.

Incredibly rich, containing more than 2,500 pieces selected with refined and encyclopedic taste, the collection that French antiquarian Louis Carrand (Lyon 1827–Florence 1888) left in his legacy to the Bargello includes masterpieces that he and his father, Jean-Baptiste (Lyon 1794–1871), collected over half a century. But there is more. Unlike many other nineteenth-century collections, separated and scattered in several directions upon the owners' deaths, Louis Carrand's collection has remained intact thanks to his farsighted decision to leave it to the Florentine museum. The absence of authentic documents—or, in any case, the lack of such documents retained by the Carrands—attesting to the origins of the pieces or to the period of their acquisition makes it extremely difficult to date their entry into the collection, and only in rare cases is it possible to retrace their origins.[3]

Even for the substantial collection of enamels (around 140), information is limited; contemporary sources lead us, however, to understand that Jean-Baptiste Carrand's collection contained valuable pieces as early as the 1840s. We can read between the lines of texts by important authors, such as Alexandre Du Sommerard, who as early as 1843 cited Carrand and other collectors, including Didier Petit of Lyon, Baron Brunet Denon, and Alexandre Sauvageot, among those who not only devoted themselves to studying the art of enamel but were also "bien munis de ses produits."[4] Moreover, in that decade in France, interest in painted enamel, particularly in products from Limoges, was steadily increasing.[5] While in 1842, Adrien de Longpérier observed that "les collections d'émaux ne sont pas encore assez nombreuses, ni faites avec assez de méthode,"[6] Eugène Piot would note shortly afterward that "les émaux du seizième siècle, lorsqu'ils sont d'une belle conservation et que les pièces sont importantes, ont un prix assez élevé."[7]

As early as 1847, French collectors' enthusiasm for enamels

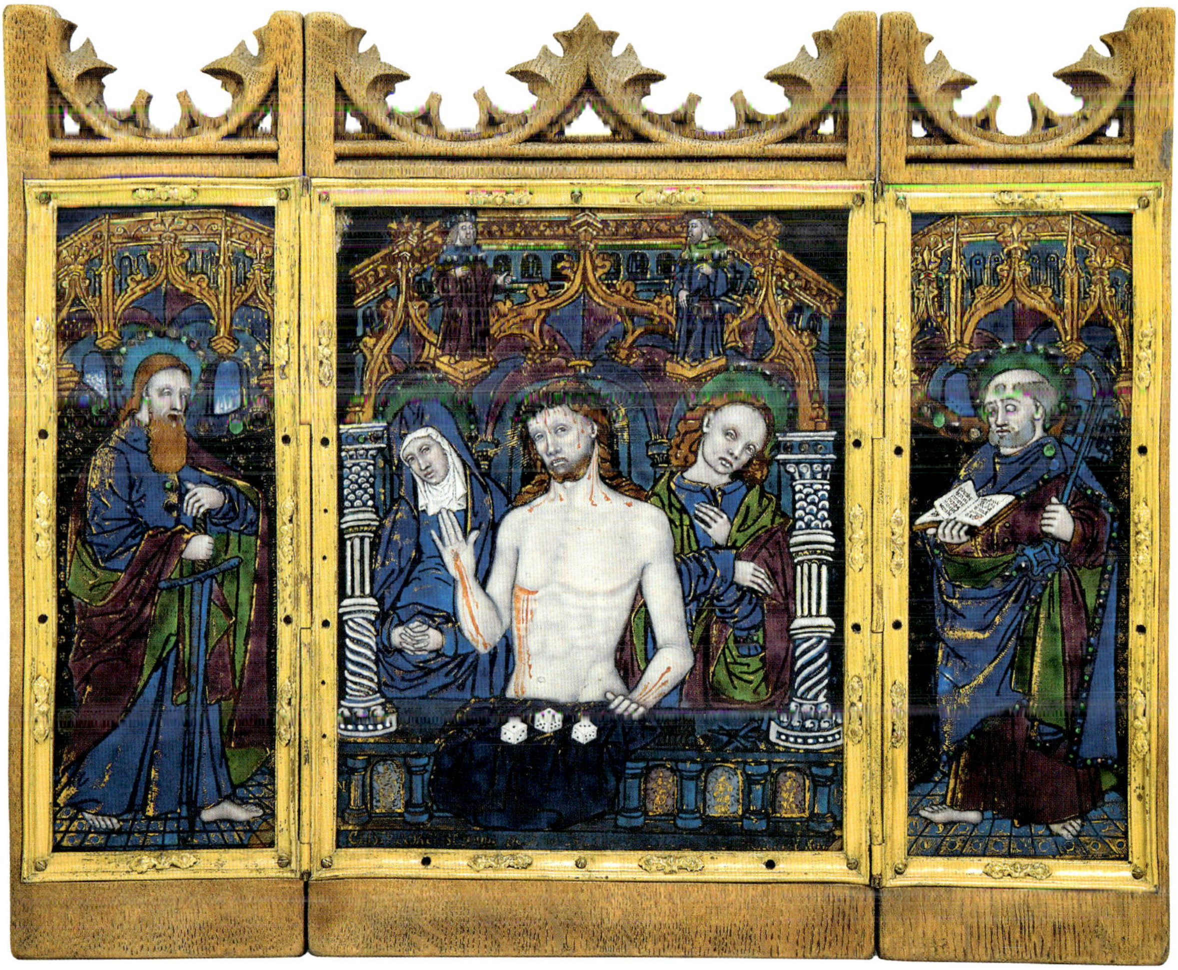

Fig. 1. The *Man of Sorrows* triptych on its nineteenth-century wooden mount

could already be said to have skyrocketed. In the *Description des objets d'art qui composent la collection Debruge-Duménil*, Jules Labarte dedicated three long chapters to enamels. One after the other, the enamellers, their masterpieces as these gradually come to light, and the respective owners of the latter are listed, and here we find noted as *chez M. Carrand* a triptych attributed to Pseudo Monvaerni, which is in all likelihood the very same *Man of Sorrows* that is housed today in the Bargello.[8] In mid-nineteenth-century Paris, Jean-Baptiste Carrand, already in possession of a collection spanning the most varied artistic genres, was one of the greatest collectors of enamels.[9] In 1852, some of the key pieces in his collection gained important recognition from Laborde: the author noted several of Carrand's pieces in the above-mentioned catalogue of enamels exhibited at the Louvre, thereby, through such a prestigious association, implicitly confirming their merit and rarity. Laborde must have seen the pieces himself, as he described the *Man of Sorrows* (no. 1187 C) and *Noli me tangere* (no. 1188 C) triptychs with a level of detail that would have been impossible otherwise.[10] Now famous, the two objects also featured prominently in the monograph on the Pénicauds published in 1858 by Maurice Ardant, another important pioneer in the study of the Limoges enamellers.[11] However, this moment in the literary spotlight was brief, and both triptychs soon ceased to feature in the press. This may reflect the Carrands' tendency to avoid publicising their pieces; they were reluctant, for example, to send their masterpieces to exhibitions, especially the enamels.[12]

Jean-Baptiste Carrand's passion for enamels also emerged in another area of his life. While he had long been considered an undisputed authority among the throngs of collectors and antiquarians in Paris, he was, with increasing assistance from the young Louis, also pursuing a parallel activity: restoration.[13] Indeed, he is mentioned frequently in the context of enamel restoration in the press at the

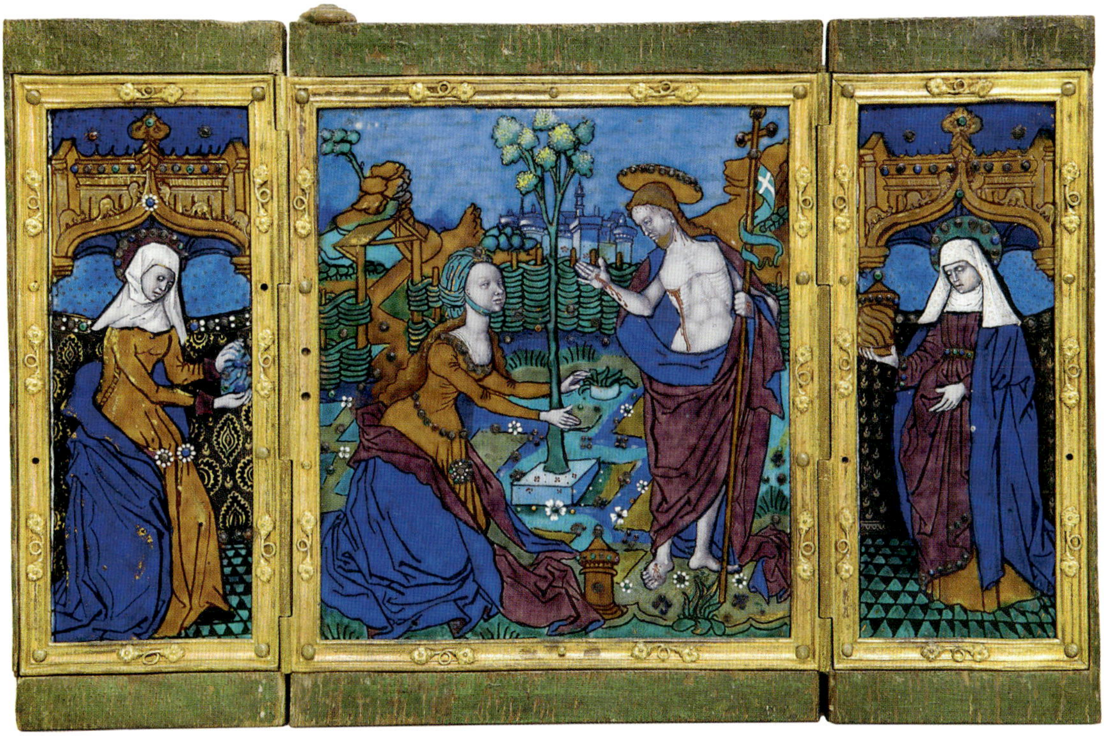

Fig. 2. The *Noli me tangere* triptych on its nineteenth-century wooden mount

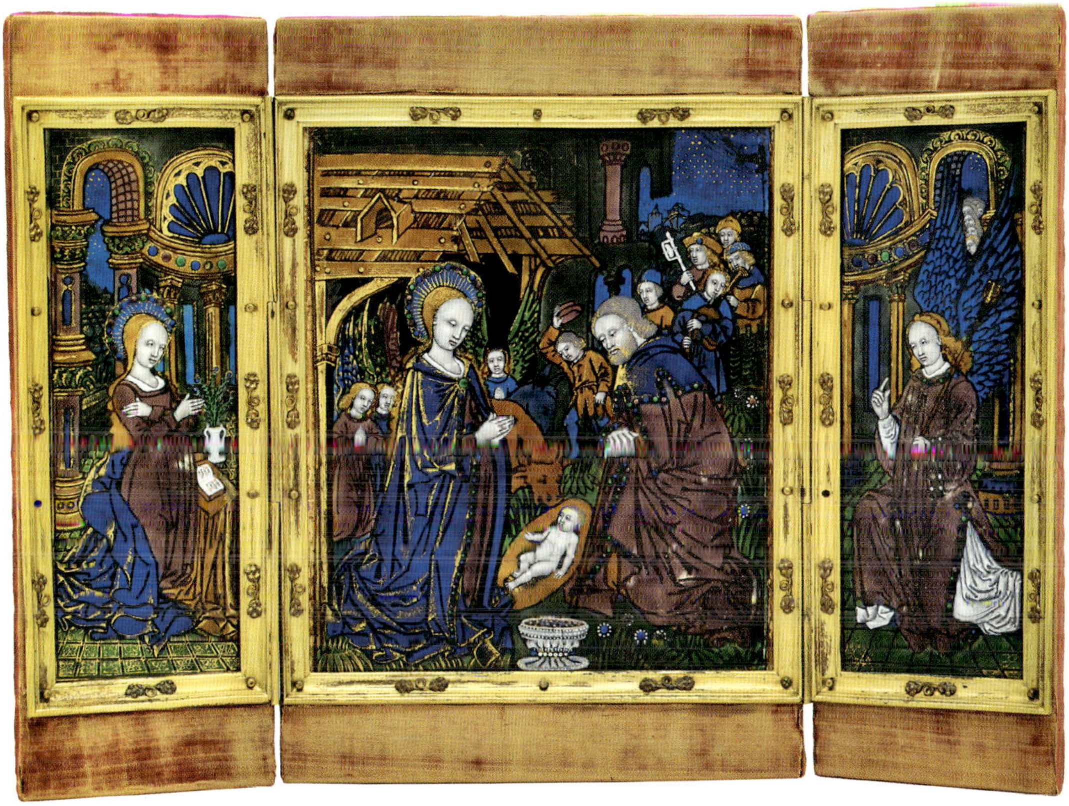

Fig. 3. The *Adoration* triptych on its nineteenth-century wooden mount covered in fabric

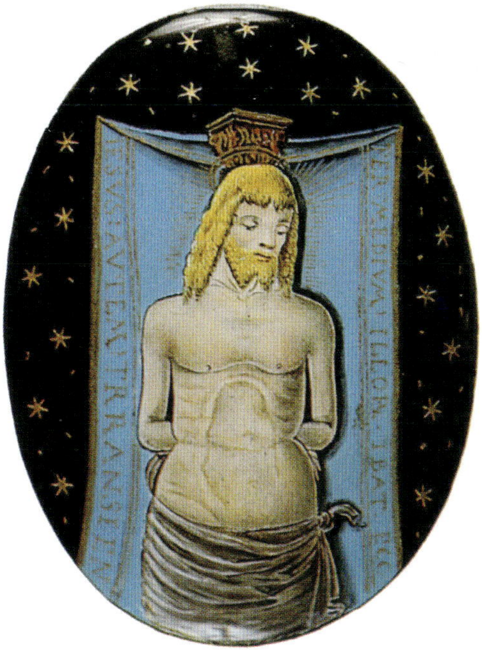

Fig. 10. Lombard enameller, *Christ at the Column*, Florence, Museo Nazionale del Bargello

Interest in Renaissance painted enamels from Limoges resurfaced in France around the time of the publication of Victor Hugo's popular *Notre Dame de Paris* in 1831, coinciding with the period of the Romantic movement. It was given a boost by the writings of Prosper Mérimée, Honoré de Balzac, and Théophile Gautier, which turned attention to the Valois court in the sixteenth century and the attendant artistic production, including enamels. Many pieces came to Paris in 1806 following the Napoleonic campaigns, but in the meantime, they were the subject of highly detailed descriptions, and enamel collecting took off.[48]

One of the first enamel collectors was Jean-Baptiste Carrand (1794–1871), who was already displaying his pieces in 1826 at an exhibition in Lyon, where he was an archivist. Between 1835 and 1850, he acquired many pieces from collections up for sale, including the Durand, Schomberg, Chérronet, Grandjean, Canino, Dava, Dreugnot, Magnan de la Roquette, Roger, Barthélemy, Monfort, Roussel, Brunet-Denon, Baron, Moser, Commarmond, Delange, Sommerson, and Piot collections. As both collector and expert adviser to Prince Alexis Soltykoff, he contributed his considerable expertise to the sale of the Debruge-Duménil collection in 1849. Two years earlier, Jules Labarte had catalogued this famed collection, giving it visibility through a publication in which he highlighted a triptych in the Carrand collection, probably the one with the *Man of Sorrows* that then came to the Bargello.[49]

Research on the history and techniques of Limousin enamels also began during these same years.

The subject drew the interest of scholars of the caliber of Jacques-Rémi-Antoine Texier (1813–1859), author of an important volume on the topic in 1842 and himself a collector and owner of an enamel with *Saint Christopher* attributed to Pseudo Monvaerni (Paris, Musée du Louvre, OA 63091).[50] Equally important contributions were made by the Louvre conservator Léon de Laborde (1807–1869), published between 1852 and 1857 and followed by, among others, those by Alfred Darcel (1818–1893), conservator at the Musée de Cluny at the time, as well as Louis Bourdery (1852–1901), a painter who had been active in the area of enamels since 1878. Working with Emile Lachenaud (1835–1923), Bourdery gathered an impressive body of documentation on pieces in public and private collections, with the idea of publishing an eight-volume *Catalogue descriptif et raisonné de l'oeuvre des peintres-émailleurs de Limoges*, but only the first volume, *Léonard Limosin, peintre des portraits*, was published (1897).

This renewed attention led to the creation of the Société Archéologique et Historique du Limousin in Limoges in 1845 (an association committed to fostering research on enamellers and their techniques which spawned the foundation of the Musée Municipal de l'Evéché in Limoges) and the start-up of the collecting market,[51] with the obvious consequence of increases in the prices of the pieces. Writing in the *Annales Archéologiques* of 1854, Texier observed that the prices of enamels had soared in the past fifteen years, passing from a few francs to many thousands for a single piece. At the 1861 auction of the collection built up over a thirty-year period by Soltykoff during his stay in Paris, the enamels were sold for record sums.[52]

The fashion for owning painted enamels soon spread to museums and public collections.

The Louvre acquired the Edmé-Antoine Durand collection (1824) and that of Pierre Révoil (1828); the pieces belonging to Maurice Ardant were purchased by the Société Archéologique et Historique du Limousin (1847); the Musée de Cluny displayed the enamels belonging to Alexandre Du Sommerard in 1844; in 1902, the Dutuit collection went to the Petit Palais in Paris. And the situation was not different outside France. The Hermitage acquired enamels belonging to Alexander Petrovitsch Basilewsky (1885); in England, where the South Kensington Museum

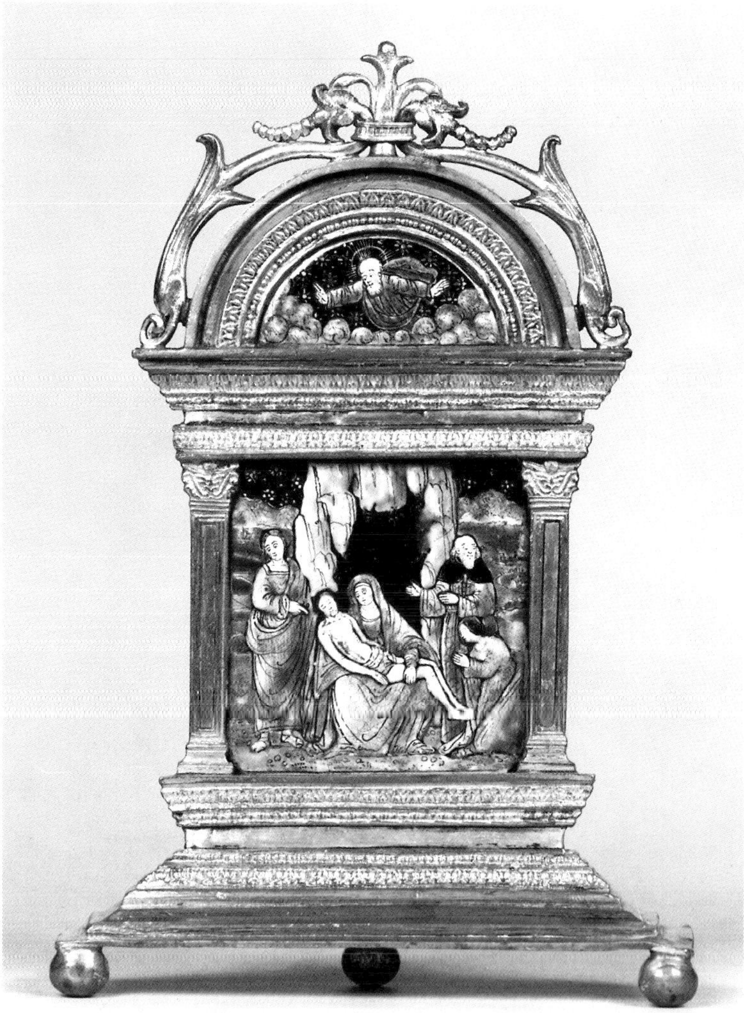

Fig. 11. Lombard enameller, *Pietà*, Baltimore, The Walters Art Museum

(the future Victoria & Albert Museum) had held a special exhibition on painted enamels in 1874, the British Museum grabbed the collection of Ferdinand de Rothschild (1898); in 1900, some of the enamels from the Wallace Collection were put on display at Hertford House.[53] As for Italy, the numerous pieces collected by Louis Carrand came to the Museo Nazionale del Bargello in Florence (1888), while those belonging to Frederick Stibbert (1838–1906) went to the Museo Stibbert, also in Florence. In 1876, a few plaques came to the Civiche Raccolte of Milan (Castello Sforzesco) by bequest from Malachia De Cristoforis, and others came from the collection of Francesco Ponti in 1895. The enamels in the collection of Placido de Sangro, duke of Martina, went to the city of Naples in 1911.[54]

Given the great demand, the originals were no longer enough; the phenomenon of reproduction began.

In France, during the reign of Louis Philippe (1830–1848), the first experiments with producing painted enamel on copper using the old techniques were carried out at the Manufacture Royale de Porcelaine de Sèvres. The first copies of the originals were made, without fraudulent intent, at a specialised workshop that opened on October 31, 1845, under the painter and enameller Jacob Meyer-Heine (1805–1879). In a volume published in 1841, Louis Dussieux noted that Meyer-Heine had recently produced an enamelled copper bowl "d'aprés les procédés des l émailleurs de Limoges" in Sévres. Meyer-Heine had worked with the chemist Charles Wagner (1799–1841), who is held to have been the first, in 1840, to

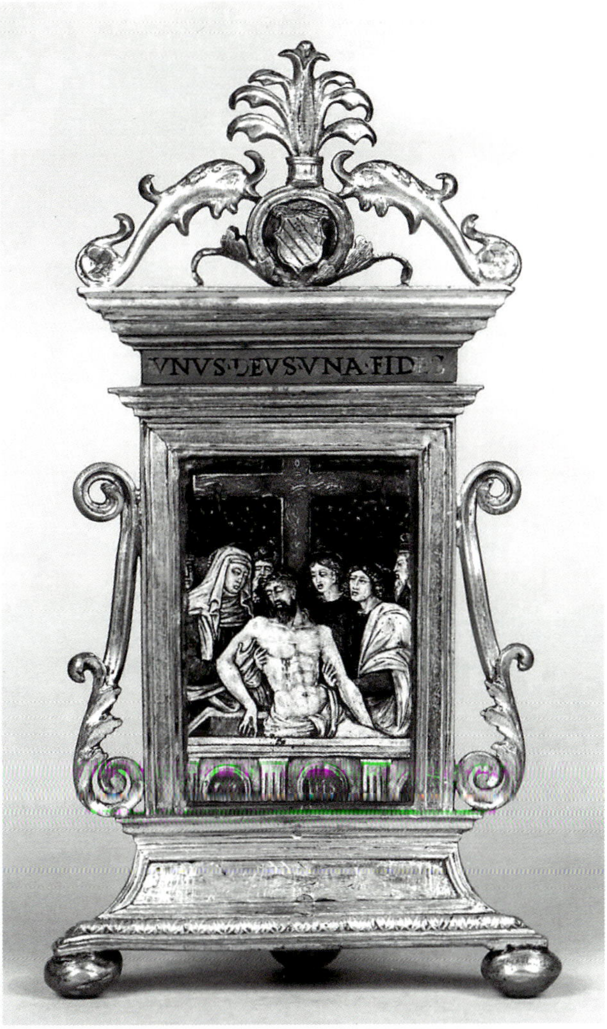

Fig. 12. Lombard enameller, *Christ in the Tomb*, Baltimore, The Walters Art Museum

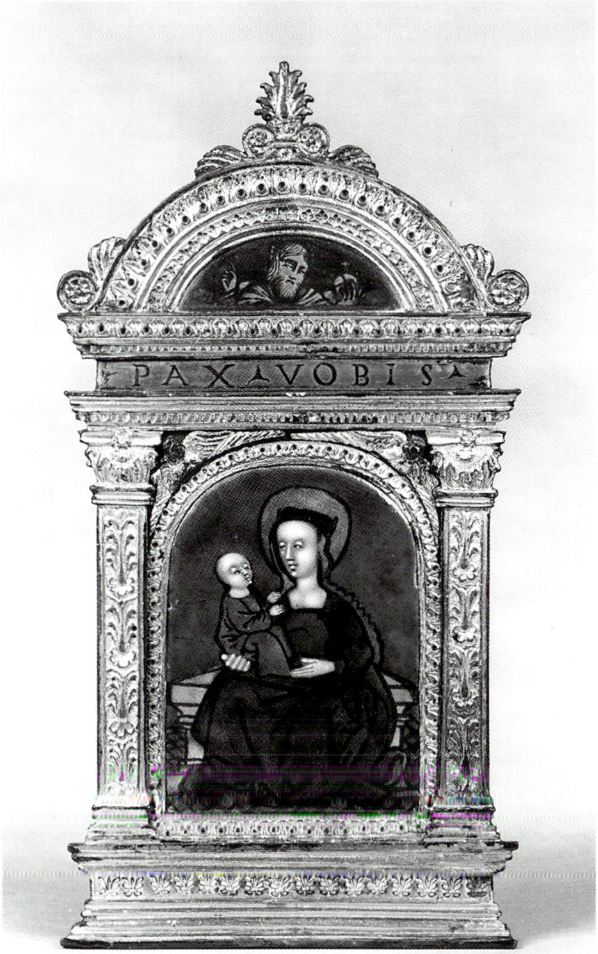

Fig. 13. Master of the High Foreheads, *Madonna and Child*, Baltimore, The Walters Art Museum

make painted enamel objects, in collaboration with the Parisian goldsmith Françoise-Désiré Froment-Meurice (1802–1855). Together, they also figured out how to make a good white *grisaille*. Before it closed in 1872, numerous masters active in painted enamel production were trained at the Sèvres workshop. One of them was Alfred Meyer (1832–1904), who was admitted to the workshop in 1858 and created very fine pieces for which he used "les paillons et les émaux de coleur translucide."[55]

The creation of reproductions was also made possible by the passionate search for old recipes carried out by French scholars, first and foremost Maurice Ardant. In 1765, Jean Baptiste Nouailher, one of the last in the line of this great dynasty of enamellers, left the recipes in his possession to his son, also called Jean Baptiste, who was a painter and enameller and who, in turn, in 1804, gave the manuscripts to François Alluaud, son of another François, director of the Manufacture Royale de Porcelaine in 1788. François Alluad brought the valuable documents to his archivist friend Maurice Ardant, who published them in the volume *Émailleurs et émaillerie de Limoges* (printed in 1844 and then again in 1855), in the chapter "Secrets recettres et procédés des émailleurs limousins." The chapter gathered four sources: the oldest, dated 1583, written by the goldsmith Dominique Mouret; an anonymous text from the seventeenth century; the recipes of "Mademoiselle Laudin" (possibly Valérie, the daughter born in 1691 to Jacques II); and, lastly, the recipes compiled between 1736 and 1749 by "Baptiste Nouailher," presumably Jean Baptiste I, son of Pierre, born in 1697.[56]

marked by “deux lettres M. P., l’une à l’extrémité droite du tableau central, l’autre à l’extrémité gauche,” and wonders if they might be interpreted as “Monvaerni pinxit.”[2] The Bargello triptych is in any case undoubtedly the one referenced by Léon de Laborde (1852) in his discussion of the production of Jean I Pénicaud. Considering the enameller “anonyme N L,” whom he held to be from Pénicaud’s workshop, he noted the two letters to the sides of the balustrade in the central plaque of a triptych that he wrote was in the Carrand collection, pointing out the generous use of gold highlights in the work, held to be typical of Jean I Pénicaud, and the architecture in the style popular between 1485 and 1510.[3] In the subsequent edition of his volume (1853), Laborde interpreted the initials N L as “Nardon Limousin,” attributing the piece to Nardon Pénicaud (an enameller who had only emerged from oblivion that year, 1853), and again mentioned the present triptych. He repeated these observations in the 1857 edition of the volume. Maurice Ardant (1858) agreed with the interpretation of the initials as N L and the reference to Nardon Pénicaud, dating the piece to between the late fifteenth century and the early sixteenth. The work continued to be attributed to Nardon Pénicaud by other scholars, with the initials alternatively read as N P and N L. In his detailed study of the triptych,[4] Jean-Joseph Marquet de Vasselot (1921) emphasised its exceptional quality but questioned the attribution. While noting a few details indicative of Nardon’s influence, he proposed an attribution to the “atelier du Triptyque de Louis XII,” wondering whether the two letters to the sides of the balustrade, which he read as “N et L,” separated in this way, might be not those of the artist (that

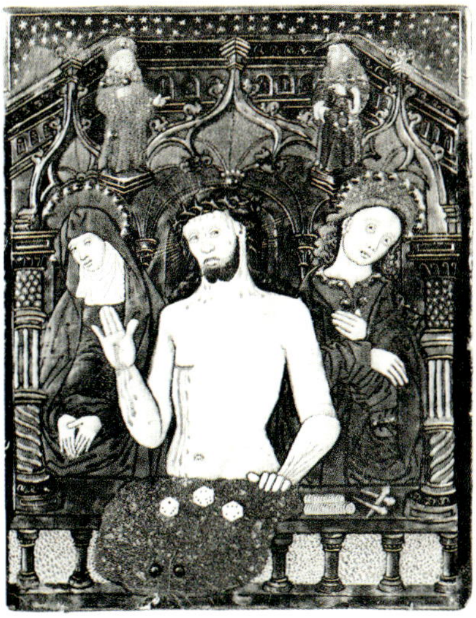

Fig. 1. Workshop of Nardon Pénicaud, plaque with the *Man of Sorrows*, Baltimore, The Walters Art Museum

is, Nardon Pénicaud) but instead those of the donors, the “signatures” of Jean I Pénicaud, Jean II Pénicaud, and their contemporaries being “tracées côte à côte.”[5] He also noted the strange iconography of placing Saint Paul instead of Saint Peter to the right of Christ and pointed out a triptych in the collection formerly belonging to Frédéric Spitzer with a central panel that reproduces that of the Carrand triptych and images of two prophets in the two side panels.[6] These three enamels are now at the Walters Art Gallery, Baltimore: the two prophets, inv. 44-645 A and B, attributed to the workshop of the Master of the Orléans Triptych, and the *Man of Sorrows*, inv. 44.438, traced to a follower of Nardon Pénicaud and dated to the early sixteenth century (fig. 1), were arbitrarily put together to form a triptych when the three plaques were in the Spitzer collection.[7] As compared with the Carrand enamel with the Christ, the Baltimore enamel (with no inscriptions) is different in a few respects: Mary’s hands are resting on her lap rather than clasped, and the marble backgrounds of the balustrade arches have no figures and are “pink and lavender and speckled with green,” as observed by Philippe Verdier,[8] who also noted the extraordinary quality of the Bargello piece and held that the two letters in its central plaque should be read as N L. Discussing the Baltimore enamel, Verdier saw the “canopy” as very similar to the one in the engraving used as the title page for the edition of *Trésor de l’âme chrétienne* published in Geneva in 1494, whereas the small figures of prophets recall those in the first printed Books of Hours. As for the iconography, he viewed the appearance of Christ from a kind of balcony as an evocation of the *Ecce homo*.

With the attribution of the Carrand triptych to Nardon Pénicaud, it is, in my view, important to add, in relation to the iconography of the central enamel, that the vivid realism of the wounded body of Christ (a body at once both tormented and glorious) portrays the Risen Christ as a bridge between life and death in accordance with a new spiritual sensibility: *Devotio moderna*. Rooted in the religious awakening that emerged in the Low Countries in the second half of the thirteenth century and spread throughout Europe, this movement championed a more intimate, subjective religiosity, with the centrality of Christ as the model for life and the *Imago Christi* now the *Imago hominis*, paradigm of suffering and the human condition.

There is a less refined, late-nineteenth-century replica of the Carrand triptych at the Museo Diocesano Francesco Gonzaga, Mantua (inv. 65) (fig. 2), which I published in 2010 and which is signed “Samson” at the lower right of the central plaque. The three plaques are in a gilt metal frame

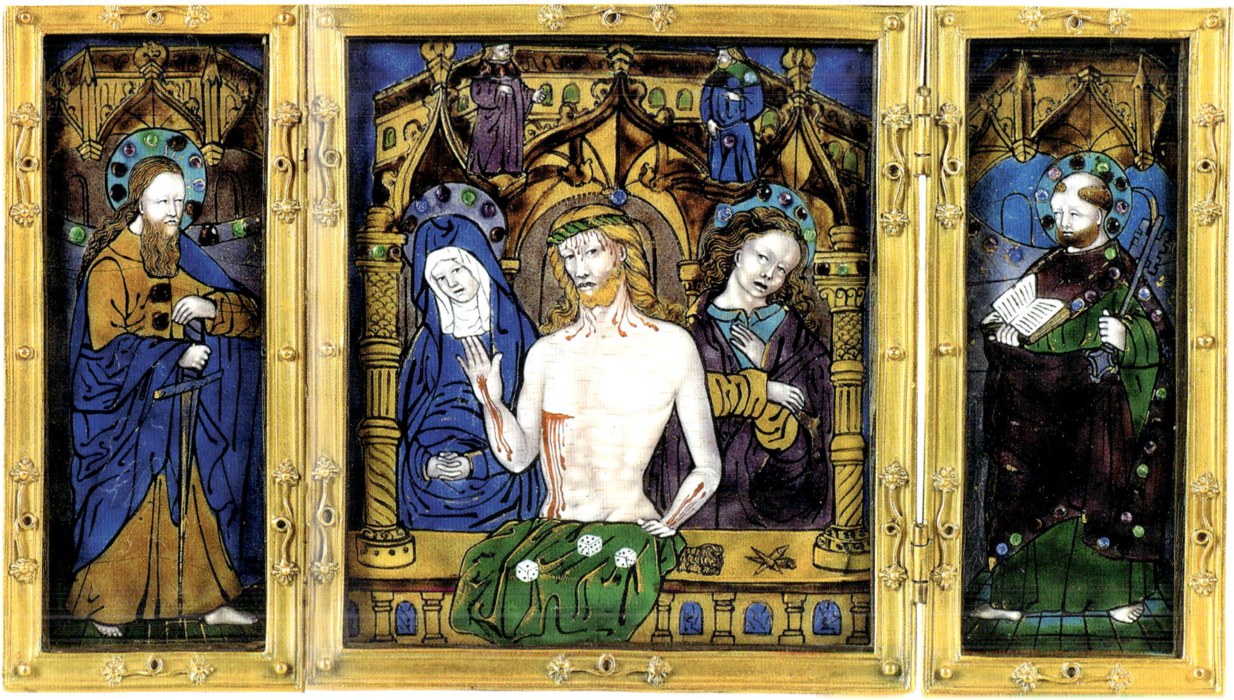

Fig. 2. Maison Samson, triptych with the *Man of Sorrows* flanked by Saints Peter and Paul (late nineteenth century, Mantua, Museo Diocesano Francesco Gonzaga

embellished with the decorative motif of the knotted tie culminating in two floral elements typical of Samson production.[9] The colouring of these enamels is, however, different (for example, the garments of the two saints, the mantle under the dice, the architectural structure, and the colonettes in ochre hue in imitation of wood), as if the enameller were working from a black-and-white photograph and had not seen the original. A black-and-white image of the Bargello triptych is found in the volume *Collection Carrand au Bargello*, which was published in 1895[10] and shows the plaques in a metal frame decorated with the motif of a tie with small leaves, mounted on a shaped piece of wood with arches in the top moulding.

We should also note that the triptych sold at a Christie's auction in December 2000,[11] attributed to the Master of the Louis XII Triptych and dated to the late fifteenth century. Here we find a *Coronation of the Virgin* in the central panel and Saints Paul and Peter in the side panels, in the same arrangement as found in the Carrand enamel, in a more modest iteration.

1. For the *Arma Christi* (which can also include the ladder, the scourge, the lance, the cross, the column, the pincers, and the sponge) and the Man of Sorrows, see Panofsky 1927; Panofsky 1953, pp. 377–378; Sciolla 1998, pp. 145–149. Paola Cordera argues instead that the money and the nails from the cross "vanished over time," as with the two letters to the sides of the balustrade (Cordera 2008, p. 51).
2. I do not know of any painted enamels of the type in question with initials in this position. It needs to be specified that Nardon Pénicaud was unknown until 1853; see my essay in this volume.
3. Laborde (1852, p. 147) provides the measurements of the Carrand triptych: 21 × 17 cm; length of side panels 7 cm. Umberto Rossi (1889, p. 19) described the baldachins as "degenerate Gothic architecture."
4. Marquet de Vasselot 1921, I, p. 168: "Depuis longtemps il a attiré l'attention des amateurs et des archéologues par l'éclat de son coloris, l'habileté de son dessin et sa disposition un peu exceptionnelle."
5. Marquet de Vasselot 1921, I, p. 169.
6. See *Résumé du catalogue* 1893, p. 58 no. 418; Marquet de Vasselot 1921, I, p. 311.
7. In the Spitzer catalogue, the triptych is attributed to Nardon Pénicaud (*Collection Spitzer* 1890–1891, II, pp. 19–20, pl. 1). Verdier 1967, cat. 20, pp. 32–35; cat. 28, pp. 52–54.
8. Verdier 1967, p. 52.
9. Venturelli 2010, measurements: central panel 13 × 13 cm; each side panel 13 × 5 cm.
10. *Florence* 1895, fig. 52.
11. "Important European Sculpture and Works of Art," live auction 6404, London, December 12, 2000, lot 14; 22.8 × 18.4 cm; side panels 22.8 × 9.5 cm; traditionally held to have come from the collection of Hannah de Rothschild, countess of Rosebery (d. 1890); there is no mention of the Carrand triptych in the catalogue.

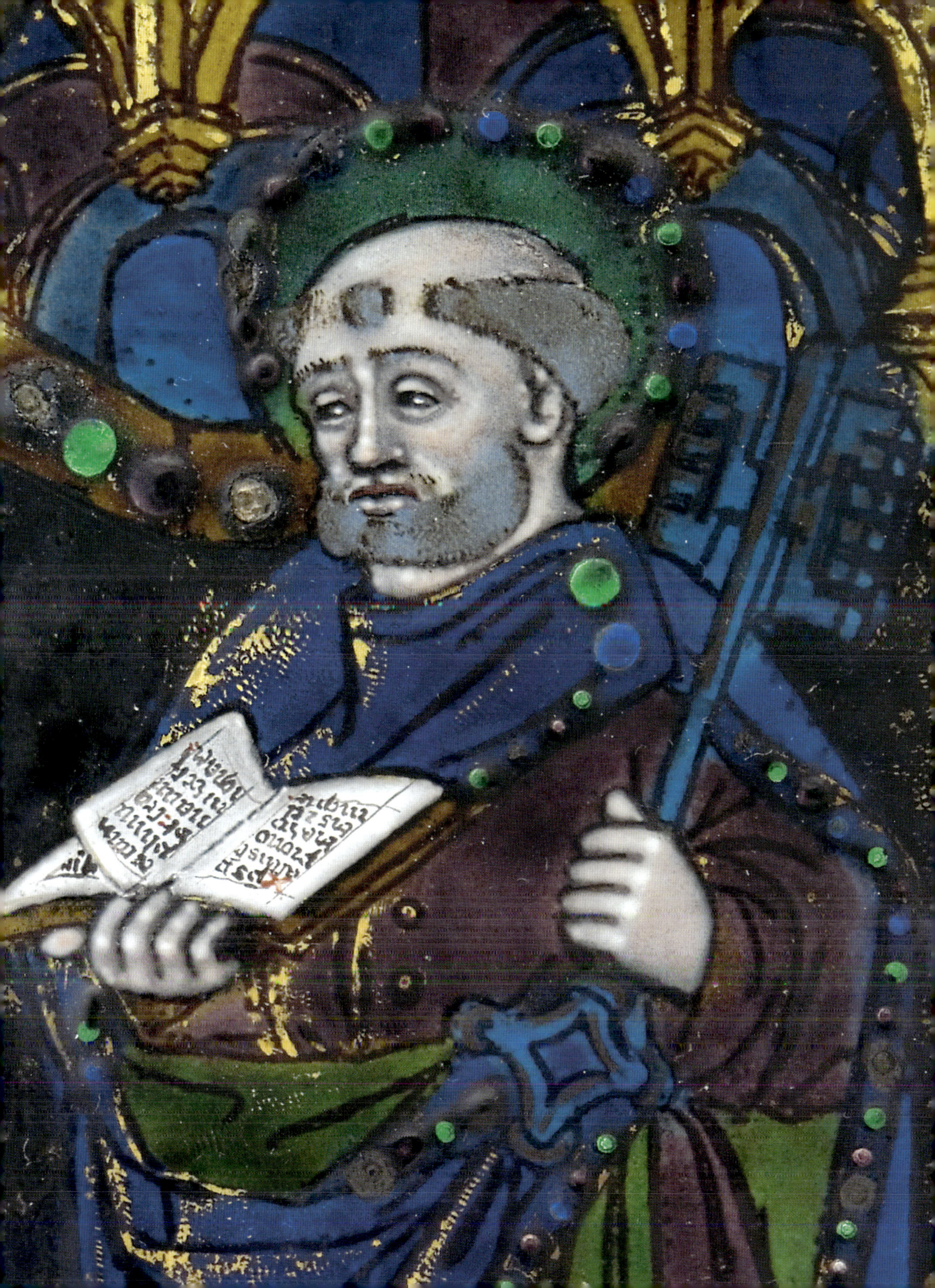

Workshop of Nardon Pénicaud (1470/1475–1542)

Adoration, Flanked by the Virgin Annunciate and the Archangel Gabriel

Enamels: ca. 1530; metal frame: 19th century
Polychrome enamel on copper, paillons, gold; frame: gilt copper alloy
Middle panel: 21 × 17.8 cm; side panels: 21 × 7.6 cm; total with frame: 40.4 × 23 cm
Inv. 1189 Carrand

BIBLIOGRAPHY: Rossi 1889, p. 19; Supino 1898, p. 283 no. 1189; Gerspach 1904, p. 16; Marquet de Vasselot 1921, I, pp. 133–134 no. 111, pp. 279–280, pl. XXXIX; "Pénicaud" 1956, p. 582; Belli Barsali 1966, p. 113 no. 49; Verdier 1967, p. XIX; Cordera 2008, cat. 8, p. 55; Venturelli 2010, cat. 10, p. 56; Blanc 2011, cat. 10, pp. 46–48.

Cited for the first time by Umberto Rossi (1889) and attributed, as with the Carrand triptychs inv. 1187 C and inv. 1188 C, to Nardon Pénicaud but considered a "much more refined piece" compared with the other two, this triptych has an *Adoration* in the middle panel and a *Virgin Annunciate* and the *Archangel Gabriel* to the sides. The attribution to Nardon Pénicaud was accepted by Jean-Joseph Marquet de Vasselot (1921), who suggested that the Bargello piece marked a new phase in the work of the enameller, distinguished by more complex compositions and less rigid renderings of the figures, perhaps indicating the "fin de l'activité de l'atelier." The French scholar also noted the triptych with the same iconography formerly in the Grandjean collection, which he attributed to the workshop of Nardon Pénicaud[1]—the enamel that came to the Musée des Arts Décoratifs, Paris, inv. Gr 5 in 1910[2]—seeing similarities between the portrayals of the Archangel Gabriel in both works[3] and finding the bowl in the foreground in the central panel of both enamels to be identical. He also viewed the white object carried by one of the people in the procession, which I believe is a sistrum, to be similar in the two triptychs. Philippe Verdier also accepted the attribution of the Carrand triptych to Nardon Pénicaud, agreeing with Marquet de Vasselot that it dated "to the last period of his career."[4] Paola Cordera (2008) dated it to the fifth decade of the sixteenth century, attributing it to either "Nardon Pénicaud" or the "Master of the Orléans Triptych," seeing the treatment of "Mary's hairline" to be "like that of female figures" by that enameller, as with the handling of the drapery. In addition to imagining illuminated Franco-Flemish Books of Hours as a probable source, she also observed that the "gilt copper frame" embellished with the decorative motif of knotted ties culminating in little roses was like the ones produced by Alfred André in the 1880s. Discussing the above-mentioned triptych at the Musée des Arts Décoratifs, Paris (inv. Gr 5), Monique Blanc, who held that it was made in the workshop of Nardon Pénicaud's younger brother, Jean, around 1525–1530, mentions the Bargello enamel, considering it to be "très proche" to the one in the Paris museum.[5] Analysing the identical detail in the side plaque, I linked the rendering of the figure and the par-

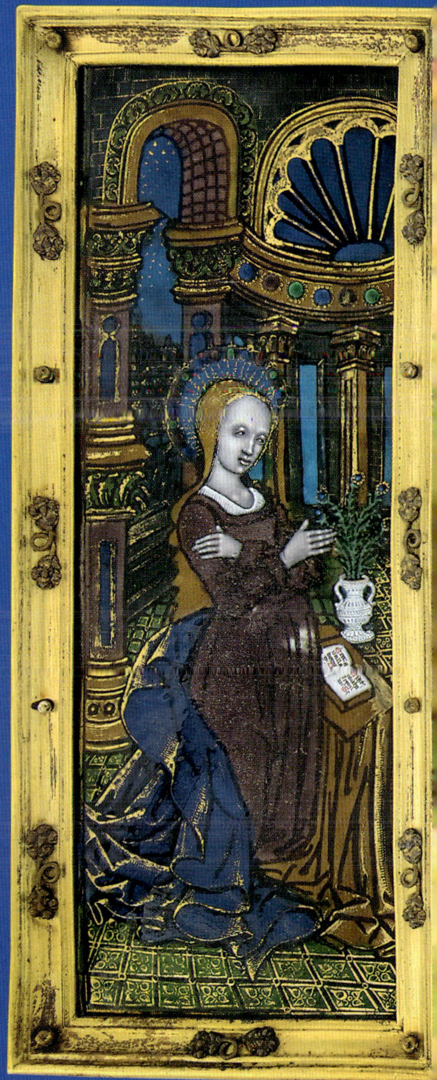

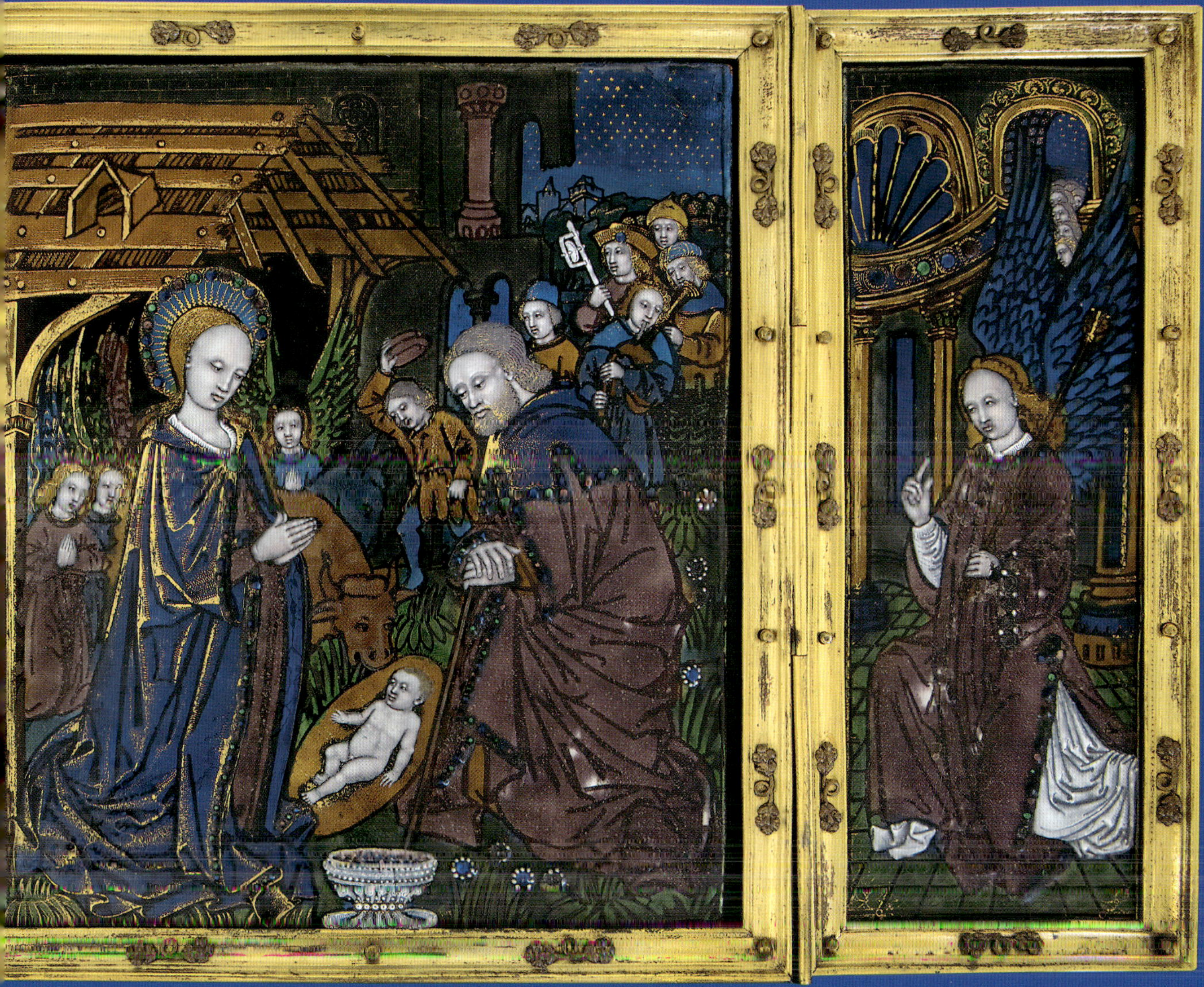

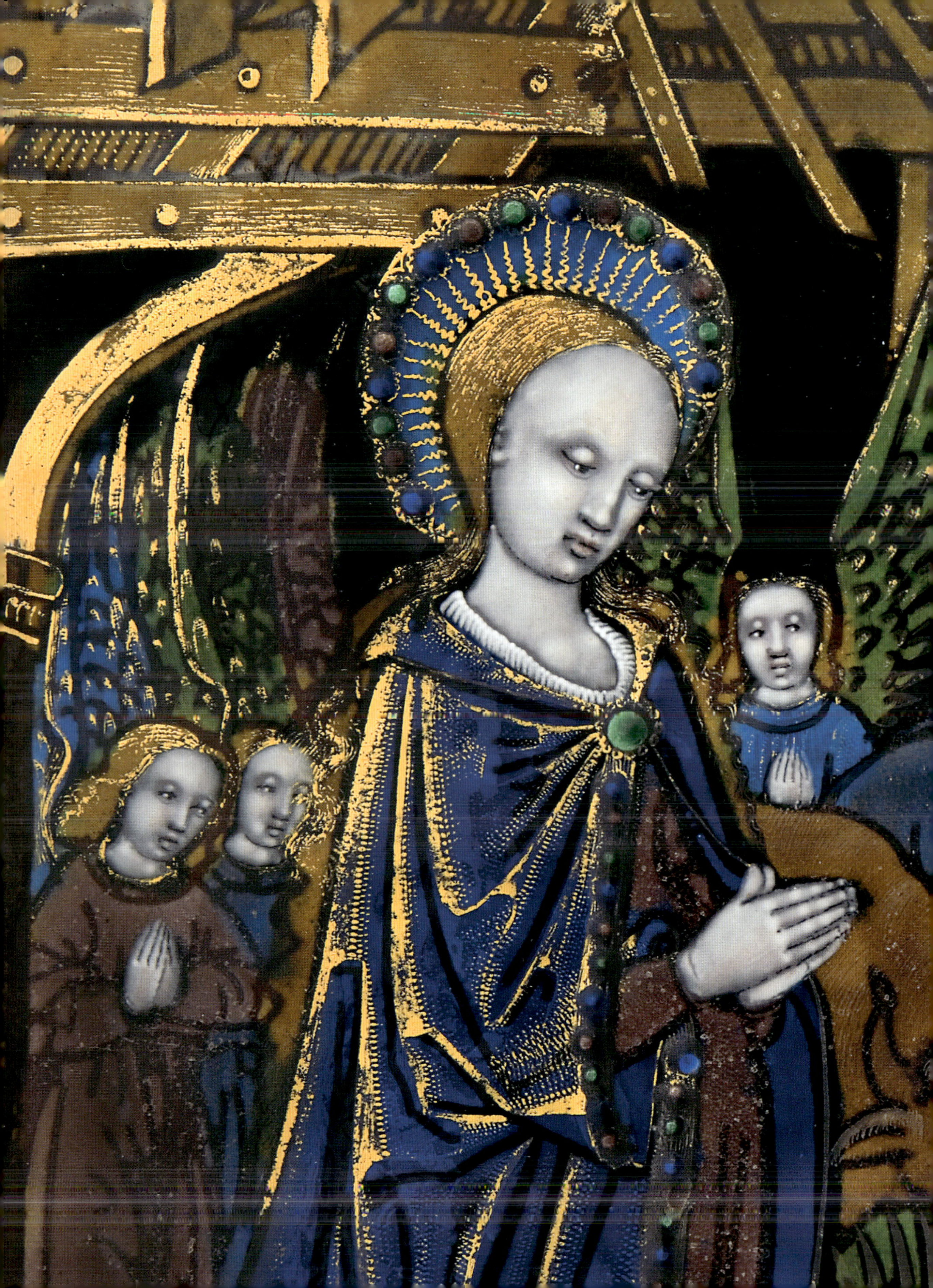

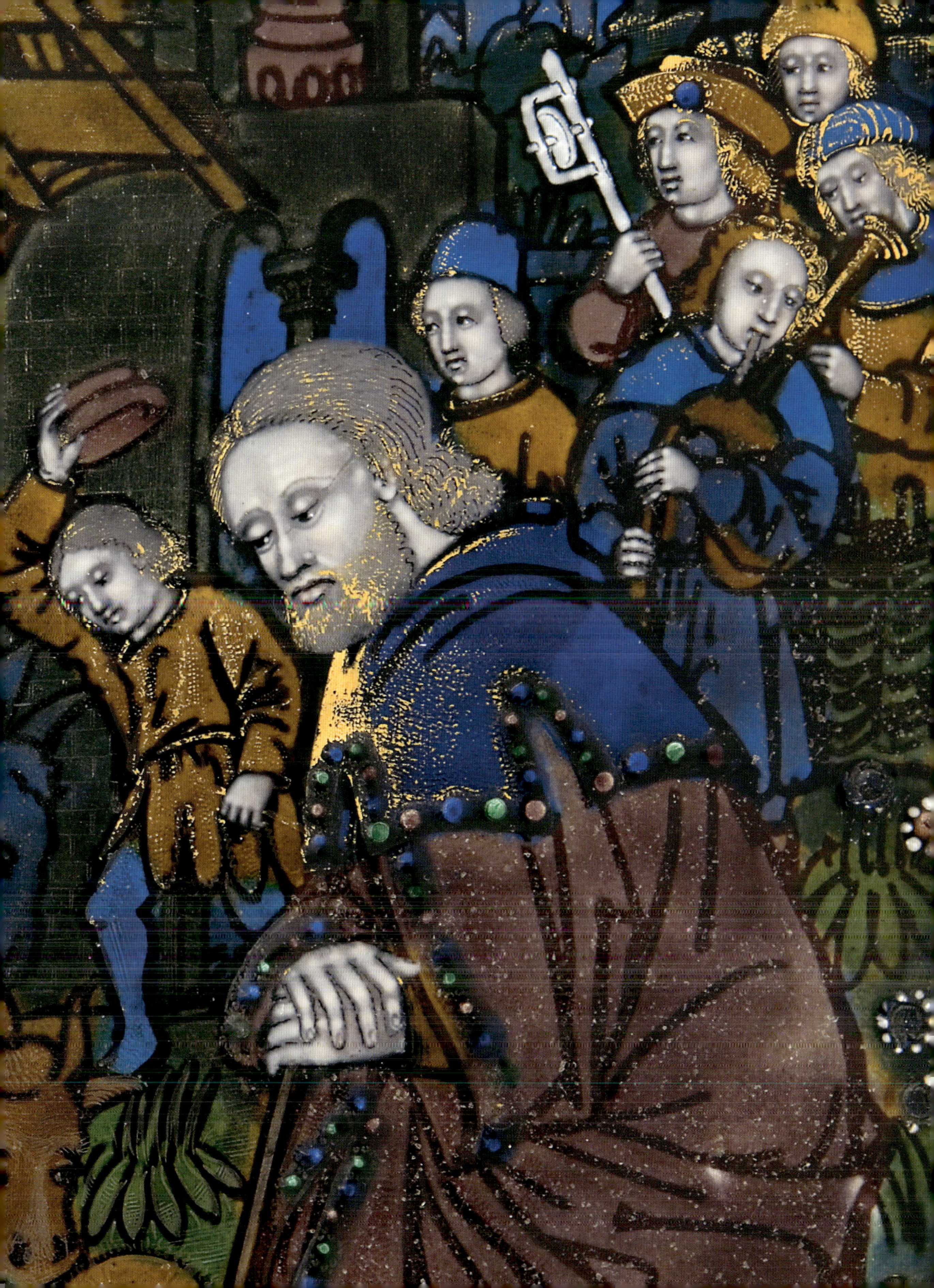

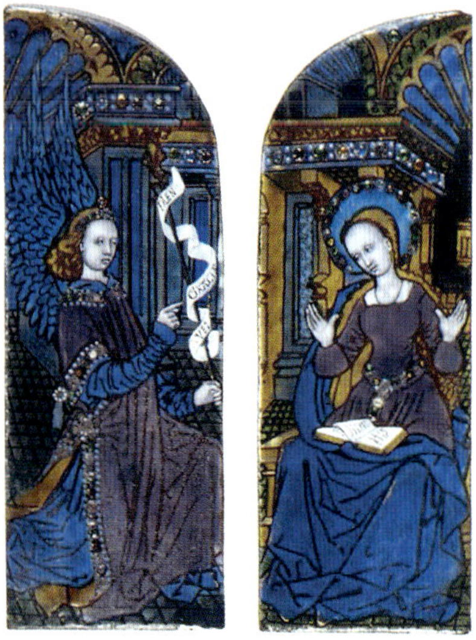

Fig. 1. Nardon Pénicaud (attr.), *Archangel Gabriel and Virgin Annunciate*, New York, The Metropolitan Museum of Art

ticular pose of the Christ Child in a tilted mandorla to the late-nineteenth-century *Nativity*, *Adoration of the Kings*, and *Circumcision*, topped by plaques with *God the Father* and two *Angels*,[6] in a painted enamel and signed "Samson" (Mantua, Museo Diocesano Francesco Gonzaga).

I would now like to add some new considerations to the above.

The middle panel of the Carrand enamel draws on two medieval texts which, through the iconography of the *Adoration of the Christ Child*, contributed to the spread of two different traditions. These texts are the *Meditationes Vitae Christi*, attributed to the Pseudo Bonaventura (probably late thirteenth or early fourteenth century) and the *Revelationes* by Saint Bridget of Sweden (1303–1373), works that were widely circulated between the fourteenth and early sixteenth centuries across a vast geographical area and from which different compositional elements were drawn. The first text was the source for the hut, ox, and donkey, while the second one was the source for the Virgin with long, loose hair, kneeling in adoration of the Christ Child, the latter lying on the ground surrounded by light, along with Saint Joseph and the Angels, rejecting the variant offered by the *Meditationes Vitae Christi*,[7] in which the Child is placed in a trough or basket.

High in quality and stylistically unified, the Carrand triptych is distinguished by sophisticated light effects created through the dense, expert use of gold highlights. Handled with the meticulous skill of an illuminator, these effects enliven the clothing (dominated by blue and pink/violet hues), hair, architecture, and treetops. These highlights are combined with a markedly decorative taste, expressed through the drops of translucent enamel on silver leaf in imitation of cabochon gems (red, blue, green) in gold settings that were used to embellish the clothing, halos, and architecture. The meticulous attention to detail is worthy of note, examples including, in the left plaque, the book open on a stand (a valuable book, judging by the gilt edges of the pages), the text of which, complete with red capitals, is perfectly legible ("Ecce Ancilla Domini fiat mihi . . ."), and the finely pleated shirt worn by the Virgin, as well as the white vase with handles and blue embellishment resting on the floor and filled with long-stemmed flowers with pistils of translucent enamel on silver leaf. Another extraordinary detail is the large white bowl with blue and gold embellishment in the foreground of the plaque with the *Adoration*, which recalls the genre of enamelled copper objects decorated with applications of minute stylised elements in gold, the result of masterful technical experimentation, which were made during a brief period between the end of the fifteenth century and the beginning of the sixteenth, traditionally attributed to Venetian production but, in my view, more likely Lombard.[8] Here we should also note the openness to Italian Renaissance stylistic elements, even if not fully understood. In each of the side panels, in fact, there is a fluted shell niche transformed into a kind of rose window open to the sky. Supported by four-sided columns with Corinthian-like capitals, the niches are flanked by monumental barrel-vaulted arches, the exteriors of which are decorated with classicising palmettes. In the left panel, the arch (behind which we can glimpse trees, a turreted castle, and other buildings) rests on fantastical pillars, pierced by impossible little windows. In the central panel, the telescope-like arrangement of the procession leads the eye to an open landscape with a fortress in the background, standing out against a starry blue sky. In the group of notables, attention has been lavished on the hats, two examples being the blue Italian-style cap worn by the young man behind Saint Joseph and the hat with a thick brim decorated with an *enseigne* (typical of French fashion) worn by the man holding a sistrum.

All of these aspects are reflected in the central plaque with the *Crucifixion* (flanked by panels with the *Way to Calvary* and the *Deposition from the Cross*) of the triptych at the Walters Art Gallery, Baltimore, attributed to Nardon Pénicaud, around 1520–1525.[9] At the lower center, in the foreground (and in the same position as the bowl in the Carrand enamel with the *Adoration*), there is a white flask-shaped vessel with blue decoration and, as with the Bargello plaque, a blue sky background that is darker above and lighter below and dotted with tiny, evenly arranged stars.

The two enamels also share the facial features of the figures, raised gold elements, and the field brightened by large flowers with open petals. Turning to the perspectival procession winding to the left, here we find a similar treatment of the hats decorated with medals, like the one worn by the knight astride the powerful, foreshortened white horse in the foreground. According to Verdier, the Baltimore enamel dates to around the third decade of the sixteenth century, a moment when Nardon could have been working with his younger brother Jean. This would explain the Renaissance air and change in style as compared with the Carrand triptych with the *Man of Sorrows* discussed above, which is marked by impassive, monumental figures set within architectural structures still broadly influenced by the French Gothic and scenes with little spatiality. Also attributed to Nardon Pénicaud is an enamel with an Archangel Gabriel with large pointed blue wings outlined in black (ca. 1510–1520) that is very close to the one in the Carrand panel and was part of a lost triptych that included a plaque with the *Virgin Annunciate*[10] (fig. 1). On both plaques, we find the architectural motif of a conch open to the sky, outlined with drops of translucent enamel on metal leaf. And there is a *Way to Calvary* attributed to the workshop of Nardon Pénicaud, also at the Metropolitan Museum (inv. 41.100.210) (fig. 2),

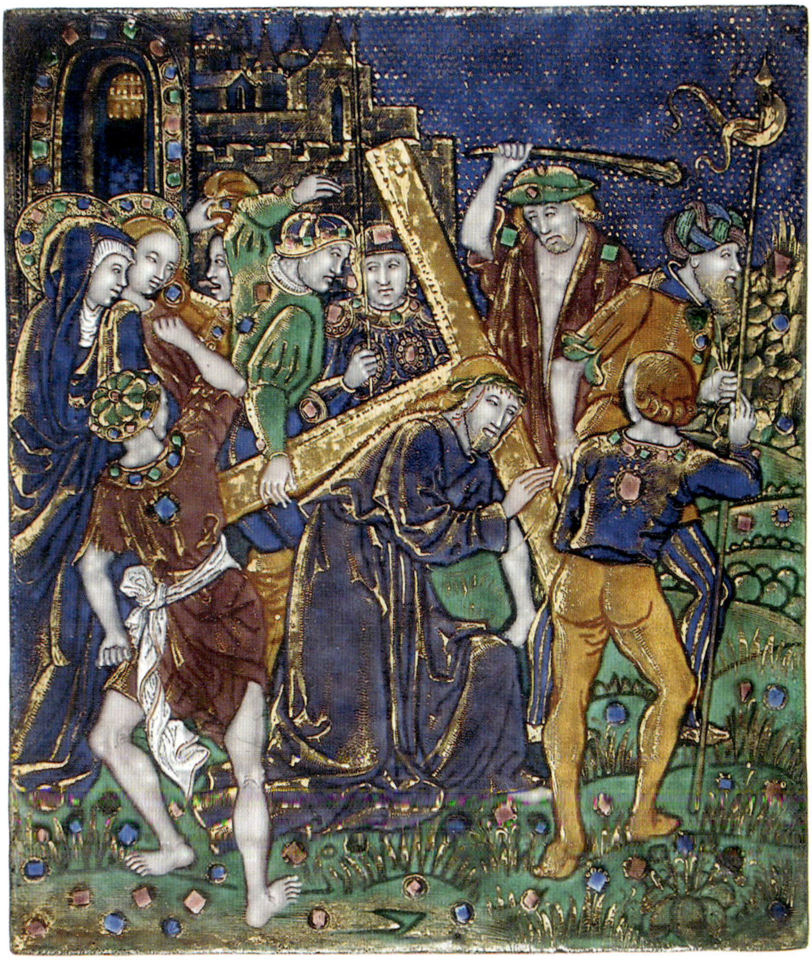

Fig. 2. Workshop of Nardon Pénicaud (attr.), *Christ Carrying the Cross*, early sixteenth century, New York, The Metropolitan Museum of Art

which shares not only the ornamental taste of the Carrand triptych but also a threatening figure holding a stick in his hand and wearing an elegant French style hat decorated with an *enseigne*, a turreted castle in the background, and a blue sky densely punctuated with small, horizontally arranged stars.[11] These details had now entered the stylistic repertoire, perhaps specifically through the influence of Nardon Pénicaud's younger brother Jean.

1. Marquet de Vasselot 1921, I, pp. 133–134, no. 111, p. 279, tav. XXXIX.
2. Blanc 2011, cat. 10, pp. 46–48.
3. In reality, the rendering of the vase in the Paris enamel seems less detailed.
4. Verdier 1967, p. XIX.
5. Aside from certain similarities in the pose of the Archangel Gabriel, I do not agree with Blanc; the three plaques of the Paris piece seem to be, for that matter, the fruit of a late composition.
6. Venturelli 2010, p. 46.
7. See Panofsky 1953, pp. 377–378; Sciolla 1998, pp. 143–144.
8. Venturelli 2003, pp. 140–141, 146–147 notes 54–58; *Oro dai Visconti agli Sforza* 2011, pp. 49–50.
9. Verdier 1967, cat. 26, pp. 46–50. Like the Bargello triptych, the one in Baltimore is mounted on wood covered with modern red velvet in imitation of sixteenth-century pieces, and in this case as well, we find the nineteenth-century metal frame with the motif of flowering knotted ties.
10. New York, The Metropolitan Museum of Art, inv. 14.40.698b, c.
11. See Rubinstein-Bloch 1926, pl. XIX.

3

Attr. Limoges Workshop

Noli me tangere, Flanked by Myrrh Bearers

Enamels: early 16th century (faces and body of Christ)?; 19th century?; restored between ca. 1891 and 1948; metal frame: late 19th century
Polychrome enamel on copper, paillons, gold; frame: gilt copper alloy
Middle panel: 19.2 × 17.6 cm; side panels: 19.3 × 7.4 cm; total with frame: 38.3 × 21 cm
Inv. 1188 Carrand

INSCRIPTIONS: O MATER DEI MEMENTO M[EI]; AVE MARIA, GRACIA P[LENA] (in gold lettering on the buildings in the side plaques).

BIBLIOGRAPHY: Laborde 1852, p. 148 note; Laborde 1853, p. 134 note; Laborde 1857, p. 134 note 1; Ardant 1858, pp. 9–10; Rossi 1889, p. 19; Supino 1898, p. 283 no. 1188; Gerspach 1904, p. 16, fig. 18 on p. 15; Marquet de Vasselot 1921, I, pp. 78, 240–241, cat. 50, pl. XVII; Belli Barsali 1966, p. 113 no. 50; Petrassi 1982, p. 49; G. De Juliis, in *La Maddalena* 1986, p. 140, cat. 49; Collareta, in *Arti del Medioevo e del Rinascimento* 1989, pp. 434–436, cat. 215; Sframeli 2004, pp. 320–321; Cordera 2008, pp. 53–54, cat. 7.

In his volume published in 1852, while analysing a few plaques with the initials N L, which he attributed to an enameller in the workshop of Jean Pénicaud, the scholar Léon de Laborde cited two triptychs in the "Collection Carrand" with the "même dimensions" ("hauteur, 0.210; largeur 0.170; largeur des volets 0.070"), which he believed should be attributed to the "même maitre." The first was the one discussed above with the *Man of Sorrows* in the middle panel (inv. 1187 C), while the other had a "Jésus-Christ apparaît à Marie-Madeleine" and two female saints placed "dans une niche gotique" in the side panels, accompanied by gold inscriptions ("O MATER DEI MEMENTO MEI" and "AVE MARIA GRACIA P[LENA]"). Writing about the latter (with "cadre [. . .] bien conservé avec sa moulure et ses noeuds"), he observed that the Magdalene wore a "costume et le turban" traceable to paintings and sculptures from the last twenty years of the fifteenth century and pointed out the "défaut de perspective bizarre . . . dans l'arbre qui, planté à distance, passe entre les bras de la sainte." Although the dimensions do not coincide (the Bargello *Noli me tangere* is 19 cm in height, whereas the enamel with the *Man of Sorrows* is 21 cm),[1] and the word "DEI" in the first inscription of the Florence piece was not noted by Laborde, the description is relevant to the present enamel. In the reissue of the volume in 1853, Laborde equated the initials N L with "Nardon Limousin" (Nardon Pénicaud) and attributed the two Carrand triptychs to that artist,[2] an attribution then accepted by critics. Jean-Joseph Marquet de Vasselot disagreed (1921), considering the style of the *Noli me tangere* enamel to be instead close to that of Pseudo Monvaerni. Analysing the triptych, he looked in particular at the blue sky in the middle panel scattered with "nuages d'or" and the gold patterns on the fabrics behind the two female saints, held to be typical of this artist,

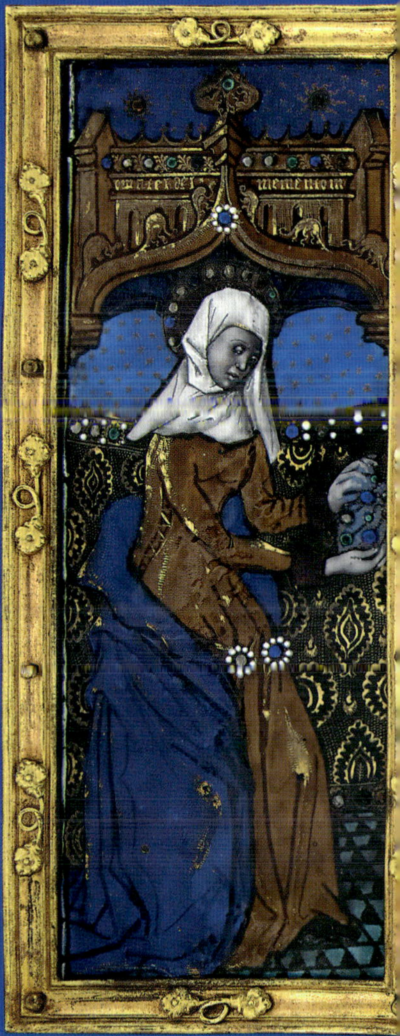

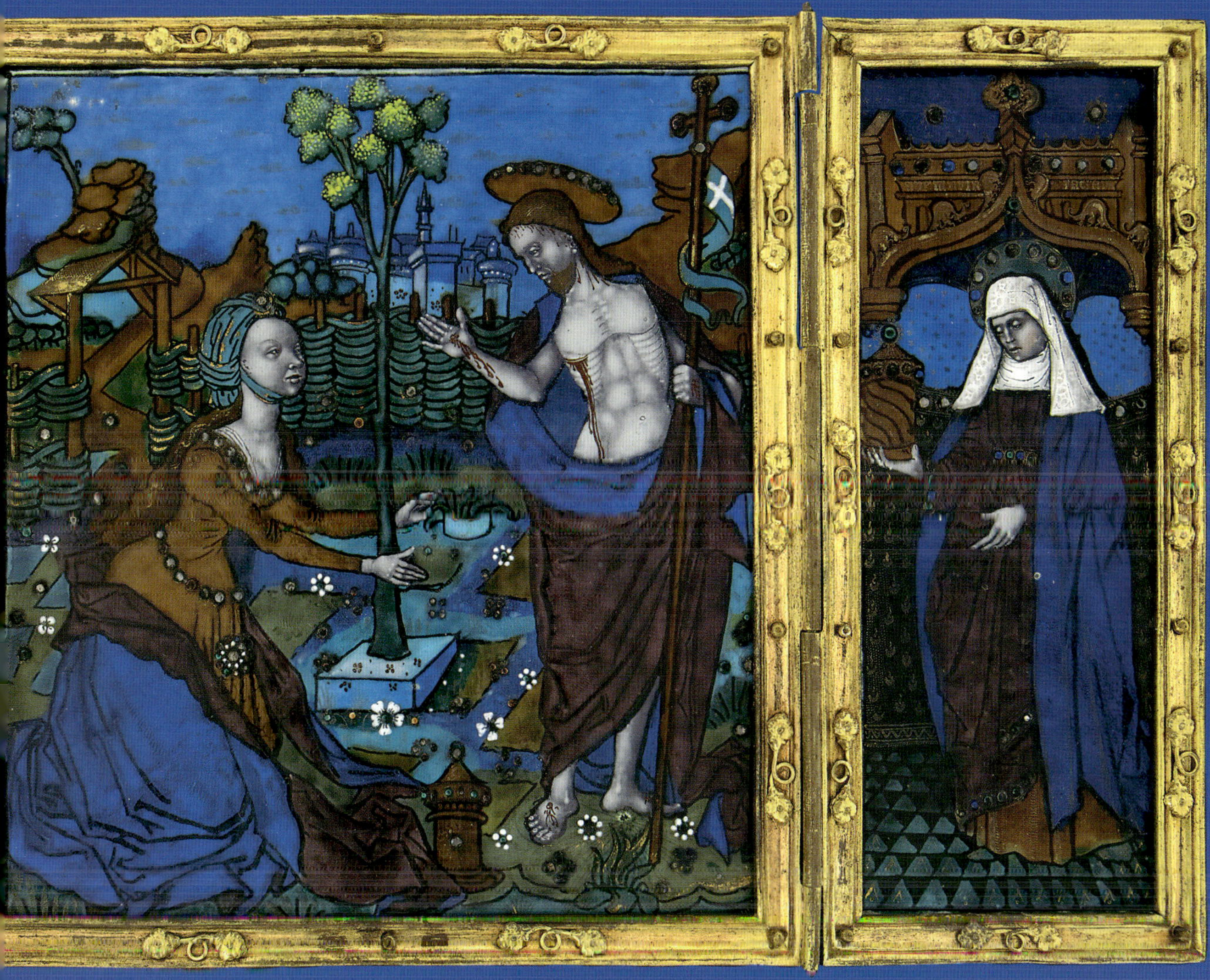

as were the architectural baldachin and the landscape with “le rocher escarpé du fond, accompagné d’un arbre isolé.”[3] For the face of Christ, Marco Collareta (1989) instead pointed to the production of the Master of the Orléans Triptych and identified the two female figures in the side panels (both myrrh bearers) as the two Marys who went to Christ’s tomb with the Magdalene. In agreement with Collareta, Maria Sframeli (2004) believed that the triptych came from the Benjamin-Eugène Norzy collection, sold in 1860. Paola Cordera (2008) observed, however, that it could not have been part of the Norzy collection (which did include an enamel with the same subject but with different dimensions and format), since it was already in the Carrand collection in 1852. She dated the triptych to the late fifteenth century and attributed it to Nardon Pénicaud or the workshop of Pseudo Monvaerni, attributing the black outline for the figures and the “drappeggio marcato e tagliente” to the likely use of engravings as a model.

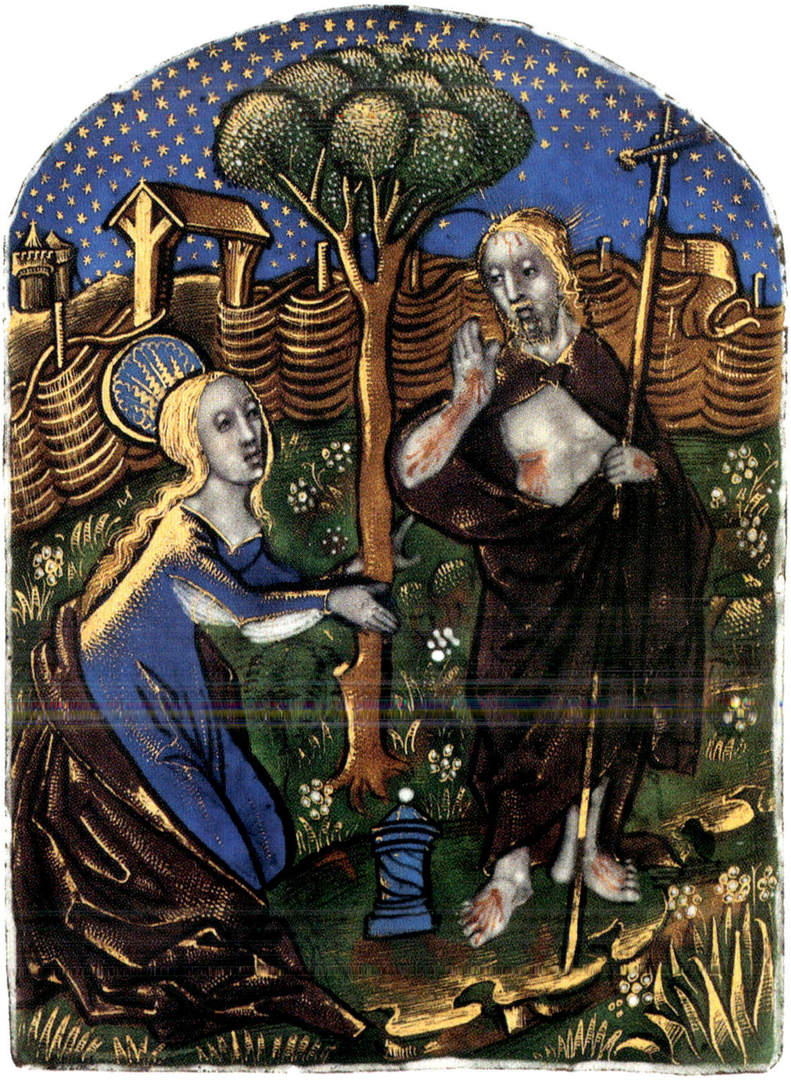

Fig. 2. Pénicaud Workshop, *Noli me tangere*, ca. 1520–1530, Paris, Musée des Arts Décoratifs

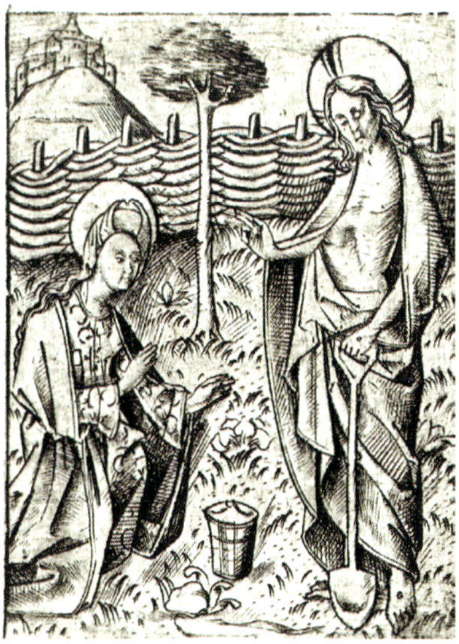

Fig. 1. Israhel van Meckenem (1440/45–1503), *Noli me tangere*

For my part, I shall add the following.

The middle scene represents the moment in which the Risen Christ appears to Mary Magdalene, who has gone to his tomb and found it empty (John 20:14–18). When she mistakes him for the keeper of the garden (where, according to John, the tomb was located), he calls her by name. Recognising his voice, she cries out, “Teacher!” and reaches to embrace him, but Jesus stops her with the words *noli me tangere* (“touch me not”), asking her to let him go and to report what she has seen, bringing the news of the Resurrection to the world. The episode takes place in a *hortus conclusus* surrounded by a fence made of intertwined shrubs, with an entrance on the left, in reference to the rediscovered Eden, and with the Tree of Life that God planted in the middle of the garden, symbolising eternal life and the presence of the divine.[4] The arrangement of the two figures, separated by a small tree placed in the middle of the scene, with the

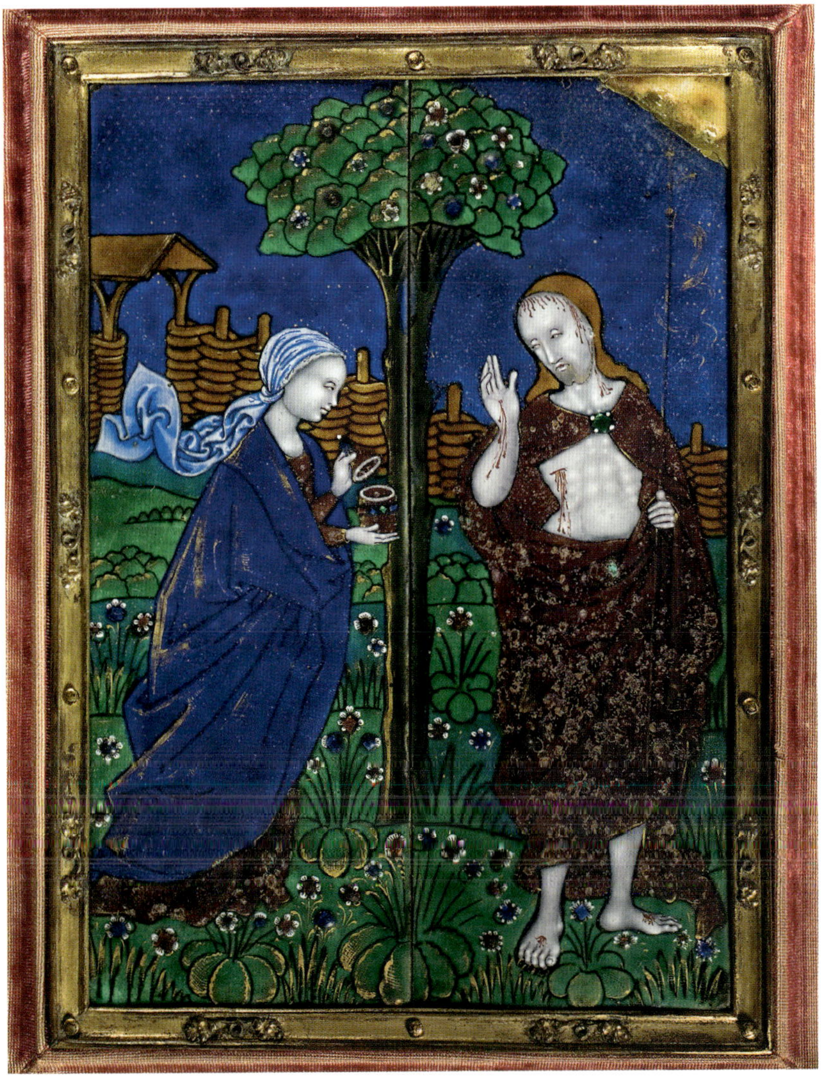

Fig. 3. Workshop of Nardon Pénicaud, *Noli me tangere*, early sixteenth century, Cambridge, The Fitzwilliam Museum

Magdalene kneeling, and the type of fence shown were drawn from sources that can be traced to the engraving of the same subject by Israhel van Meckenem (1440/45–1503) (fig. 1), in which we find Christ the gardener, spade in hand, the Magdalene wearing a turban-like hat, and a castle in the background. Another possible reference is an engraving by Martin Schongauer (ca. 1480) of Christ the Redeemer holding a standard. For the position of the saint's arms, reaching toward Christ (but correctly showing both on the side of the trunk of the tree that divides the scene), there is a miniature by Jean Mansel (1450–1475) in the *Fleur des histoires* (Paris, Bibliothèque nationale de France, ms. Français 56, fol. 57), in which we also find the generous folds of the woman's mantle arranged on the ground and a prominently placed large vessel for perfumed ointments. This solution had already been used in earlier miniatures, one example being the sheet in the *Biblia Pauperum* attributed to the Master of the Hours of Margaret of Cleves, around 1405 (London, British Library, Kings ms. 5, fol. 23). The square background of this miniature can be traced to translucent enamels on silver, such as the ones in the diptych traced to Paris, around 1325–1360, preserved at the Louvre (inv. OA 11334),[5] with the *Noli me tangere* in the inner left panel, where the wrists and forearms of the Magdalene, depicted in the foreground, seem to rest on the trunk of a slender tree.

One of the most interesting enamels with this subject is the small piece (11 × 8.5 cm) at the Musée des Arts Décoratifs, Paris (fig. 2). Part of a series of four plaques with episodes from the *Life of Christ* (inv. 21127 b, c, d, e) attributed to the workshop of Pénicaud and dated around 1520–1530,[6] it might have been known to the artist who made the Carrand enamel. Here we find a similar fence with an entrance with a peaked roof, a large tower-like covered vessel in the foreground, and a tree in the middle of the garden, behind Christ and the Magdalene, the trunk of which is mistakenly depicted between the saint's arms, a detail clumsily emphasised in the Florence plaque.

At this point, we can bring in other pieces traced to Nardon Pénicaud and his workshop. The first is a panel that was created by fitting together two enamels that once formed a diptych, put into a single metal frame decorated with the usual foliate tie motif, probably at the end of the nineteenth century (Cambridge, Fitzwilliam Museum, inv. M.10-1938) (fig. 3). Attributable to the workshop of Nardon Pénicaud, it shows the Risen Christ holding a standard, as in the plaque at the Musée des Arts Décoratifs, Paris, a fence quite similar to the one in the Carrand enamel, and a tree in the middle of the scene behind the figures, half on the left plaque and

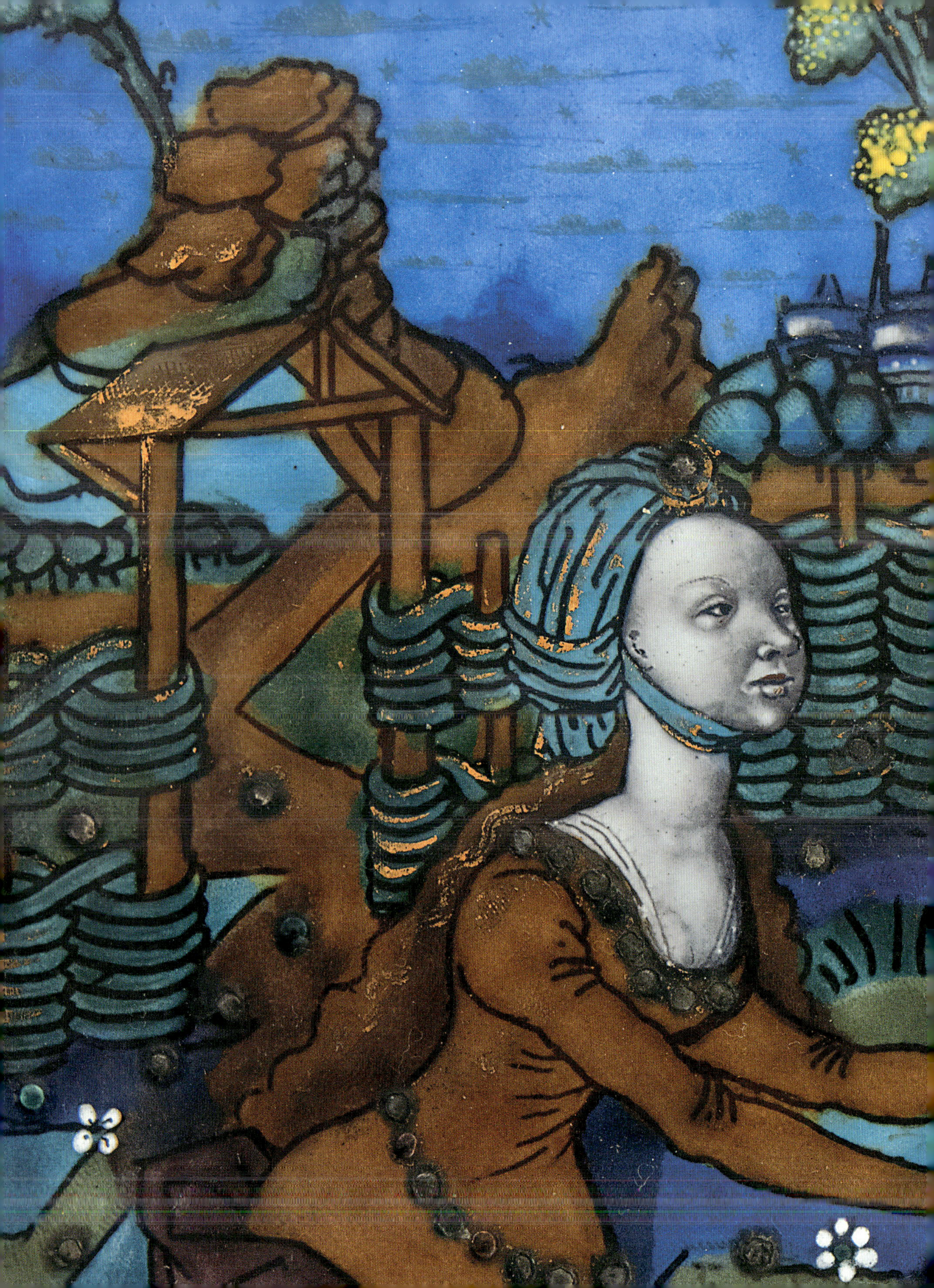

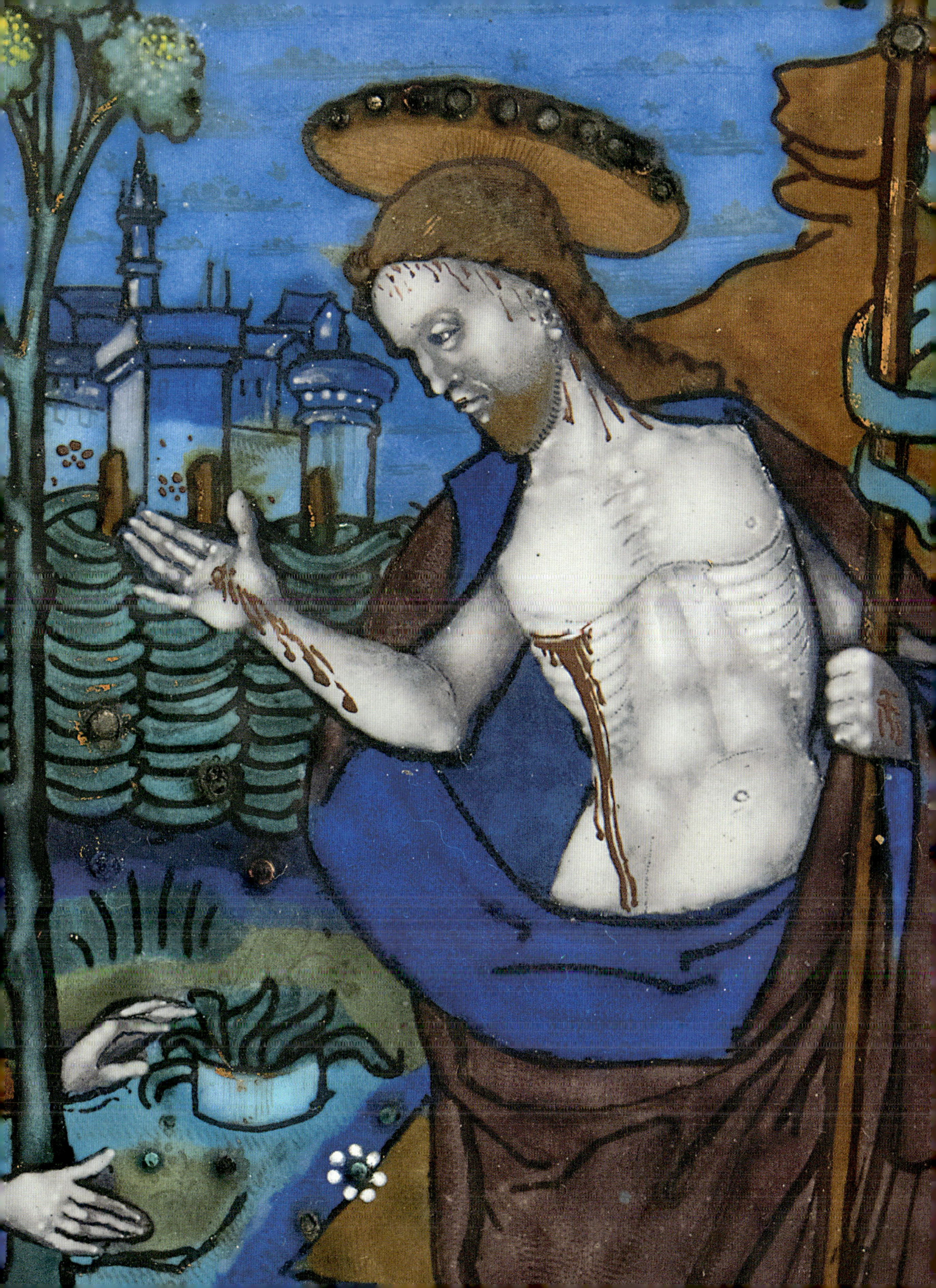

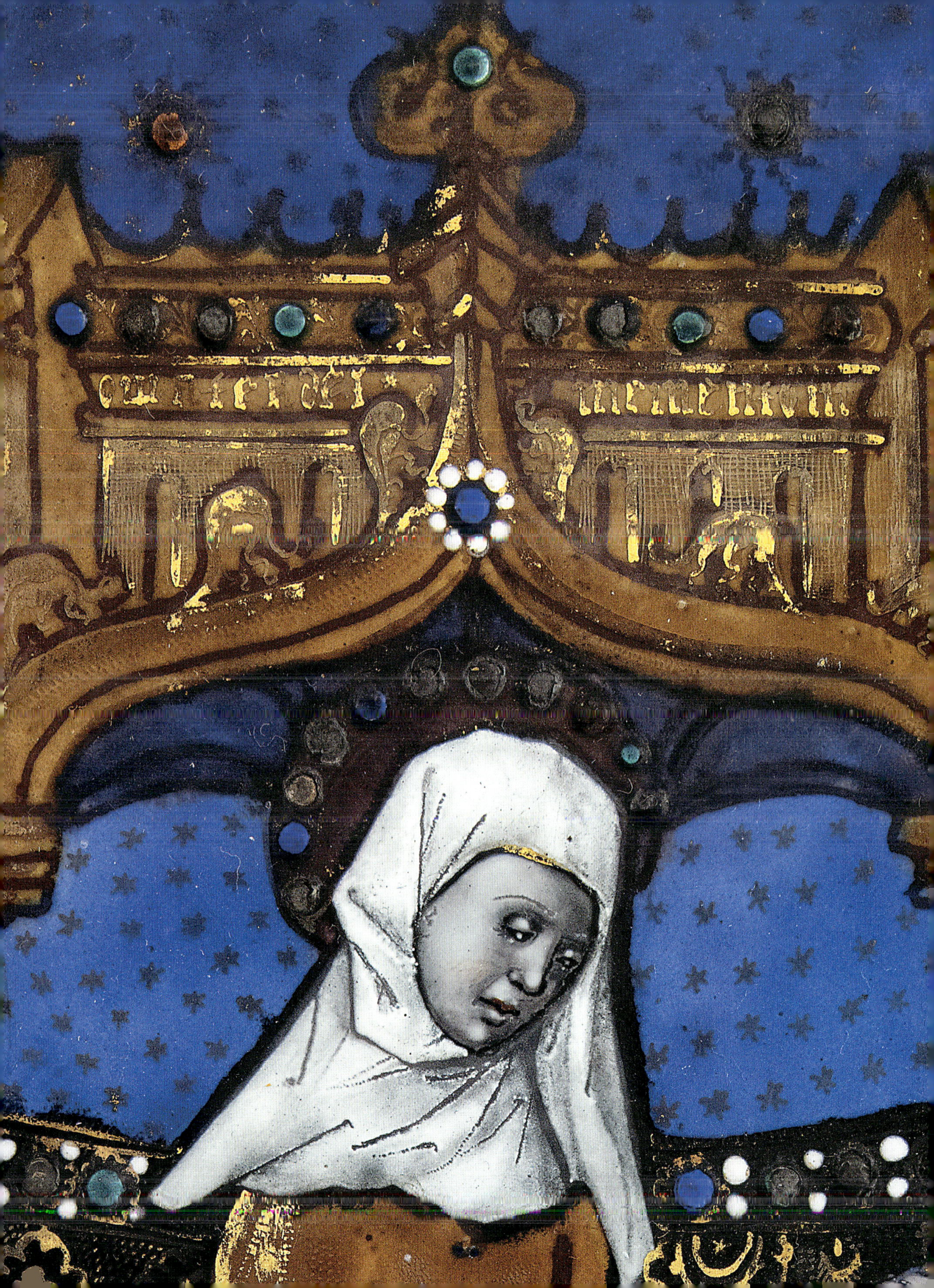

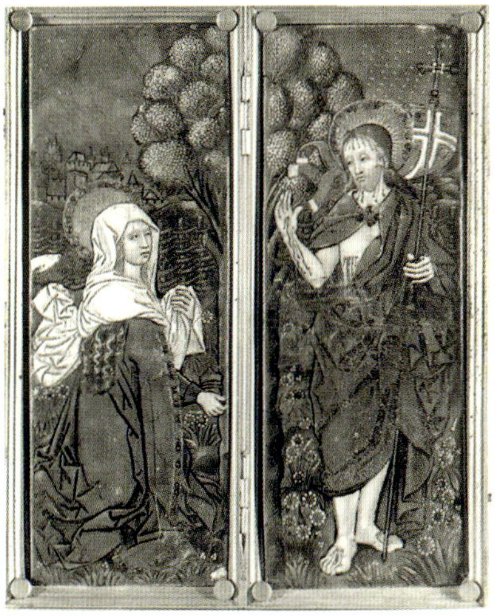

Fig. 4. Nardon Pénicaud, *Noli me tangere*, early sixteenth century, formerly Czartoryski collection

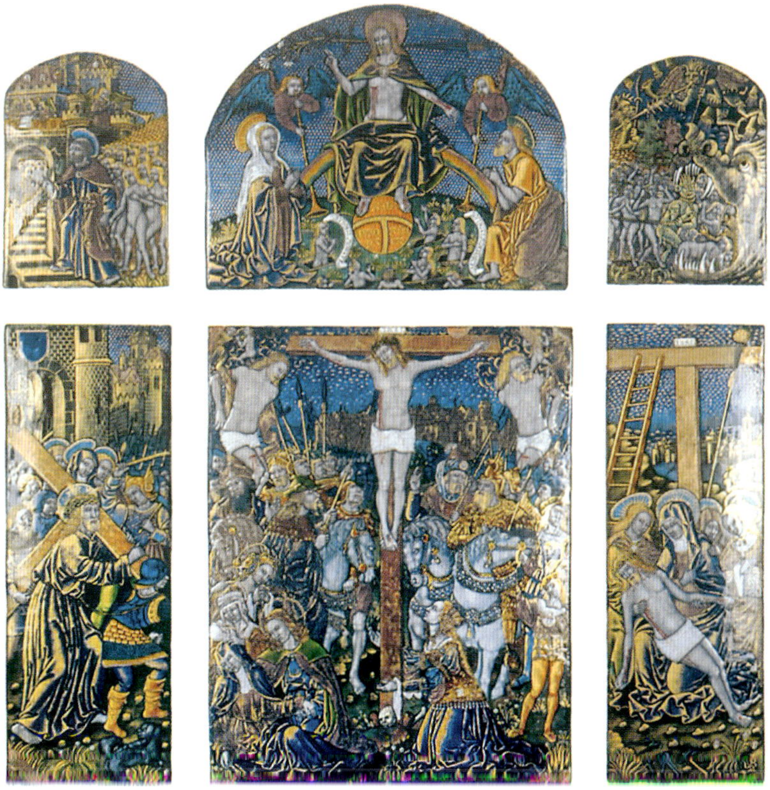

Fig. 5. Pénicaud Workshop (Jean I?), *Crucifixion*, first part of the sixteenth century, Granada, Museo de Bellas Artes

half on the right. The Magdalene is standing and holds a small open jar in her hands.

The second work is a diptych, originally in the Czartoryski collection (Castle of Gołuchów) and lost during World War II, attributed directly to Nardon Pénicaud (fig. 4).[7] I believe that this was the piece displayed at the 1867 World Exposition in Paris.[8] Here Christ is holding a standard and displays the stigmata, and the tree is again divided between the two halves of the diptych, but in this case, the strong trunk is solidly placed on the plaques' lower edge.

Lastly, the enamel with the *Crucifixion* in the *Triptych of the Gran Càpitan* (Granada, Museo de Bellas Artes, inv. CE0001), attributable to the Pénicaud family (possibly Jean I), is marked by the same mistake as the Carrand enamel, with the Magdalene shown kneeling in the foreground on the right, her arms in this case on either side of the cross, instead of the tree (fig. 5).

Partly in light of the last four pieces described above, although the middle enamel of the Bargello triptych seems convincing in terms of iconography, the style and technique used for this plaque, as with the two side panels with the myrrh bearers, are, in my view, utterly implausible, to the point of excluding the attributions to Nardon Pénicaud and his workshop or at least accepting them only in part.

The three plaques, which are particularly flat and have a thick, grayish counterenamel, are filled with inaccuracies, strange stylistic combinations, errors in the dimensions of and relations between elements, inconsistencies, and sloppiness. Examples include Christ's beard, hair, and halo; the childish framing of the grassy surface of the garden and rendering of the shadow of the surprising plinth beneath the tree; the definition of the top moulding of the baldachins using a dark line that extends beyond the shape of the structure; and the different handling of the drapery behind the myrrh bearer on the left, where it touches the floor, itself composed of strange scale-like blue and light blue tiles. There are also numerous compositional distractions (the position of the Magdalene's arms), clumsy formal renderings (the left hand of the myrrh bearer in the left panel), and meaningless details (the little red flowers on the walls of the castle in the background; the white flowers with four or five large petals placed at random points in the composition). All are in contrast with Limousin production in around 1500, especially that traceable to Nardon Pénicaud, further including the flat, monotone fields of colour, dominated by a strange shade

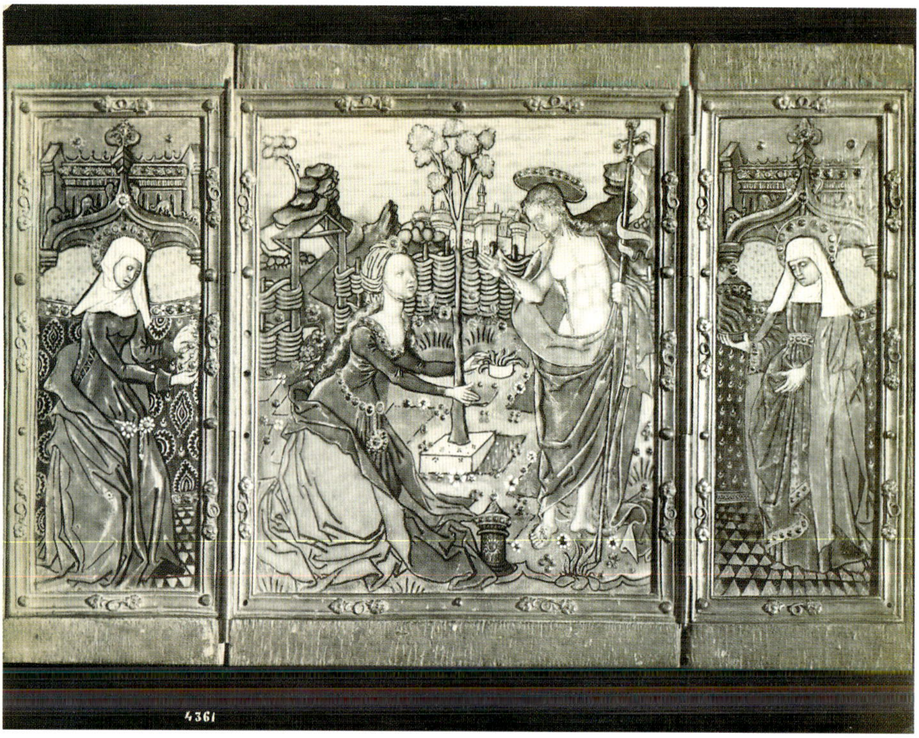

Fig. 6. The *Noli me tangere* triptych photographed by Fratelli Alinari, 1891

of blue that was used for Christ's standard (which is normally white), the Magdalene's head covering, the field, the fence, the rocks and the trees, and even to cover the small golden clouds in the sky. The way all the elements have been outlined with a thick, black, unmodulated line is equally inadmissible. And there are even historical inconsistencies in the rendering of some of the clothing. In the Magdalene, we see this in the extremely tight sleeve, especially at the upper arm and wrist, and the belt worn low around the hips, and, in the myrrh bearer at left, the emphasis of the chest and the opening of the garment along the side—all details consistent with Romanticism but not the period of Nardon Pénicaud. The brocade drapery in the niches also seems to be a modern interpretation of the past. In the left panel, the fabric pairs the wheel pattern in Pénicaud enamels with the large, ogival link patterns in Italian Renaissance fabrics, making them larger and omitting the typical accompanying foliate ribbons. As for the fabric in the other side panel, here we find the upside down flame motif from the plaque with Saint Peter in the Carrand triptych with the *Man of Sorrows*, now in a more rigid arrangement and without the sinuous vertical bands found in the original pattern, almost as if inspired by the little motifs tidily reiterated in staggered horizontal rows typical of early-nineteenth-century textiles.

It needs to be noted, however, that the renderings of the body of Christ and the faces of the two myrrh bearers in the side panels and the Redeemer himself are of a different, higher quality, one that might justify attribution to Nardon Pénicaud and his workshop, to which we can also trace the freely scattered large, daisy-like flowers with a drop of enamel on metal leaf in the center.

The hypothesis we can formulate based on the above is that we might be dealing with a restoration and/or reworking of Renaissance enamels that survived only in fragments. However, it is also possible that all three plaques were made in the nineteenth century (before 1852) in emulation of Limousin production from the milieus of Nardon Pénicaud and Pseudo Monvaerni.

Amid so many question marks, what instead seems certain is that modifications were made between the end of the nineteenth century and 1948. This is revealed by close comparison of the black-and-white Alinari photo (presumably around 1891; published in Gerspach 1904 and again in Marquet de Vasselot 1921, II) (fig. 6) and the enamel at the Bargello today, the current appearance of which is documented in a black-and-white photo preserved in the museum's photographic archive and dating to around

1948.[9] In the Alinari photo, Christ has no beard, and his hair is different, more wavy and natural, and the folds in the Magdalene's garment are more complex. The other details revealed to have been changed include the plinth beneath the tree, which seems to have been entirely white, and the shadow cast on its right, which was not made up of two bands of colour. In the Alinari photo, we also see that the ointment jar was decorated with a radiant motif that is now lost, the rocks in the background were more detailed, and the little gold clouds in the sky were clearly visible. Already present, however, were the thick, dark outlines, the inconsistent white flowers with four or five petals on the field, and the smaller ones on the castle. And we can still see daisy-like flowers in the style of Nardon Pénicaud, dotting the road leading from the opening in the fence and the fence itself, which were later concealed by light blue or brown veils of enamel.

Although it does not resolve the matter of attribution, a triptych in painted enamel on copper (fig. 7) that went up for auction in 2016 (of moderate quality and considered "possibly 17th/18th C. Limoges")[10] sheds further light on the state of the Carrand enamel attested by the Alinari photo (fig. 6). In it, we see the Redeemer wrapped in a red mantle and holding a white standard, the slender tree planted on the white plinth, the daisy-like flowers with red and blue paillons scattered here and there, and small golden clouds in the sky.

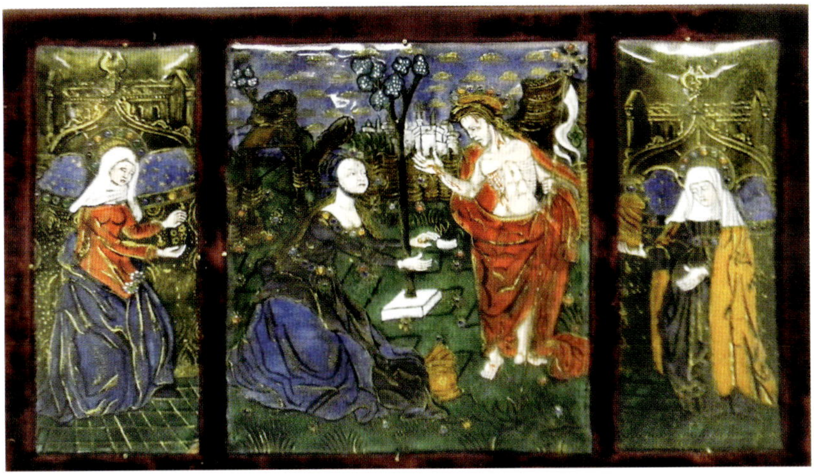

Fig. 7. Limoges? triptych with the *Noli me tangere*, Plainville, CT, Sale Winter Associates Inc. 2016

1. Marquet de Vasselot (1921, I, p. 241) reports the following measurements: "H. 0.187; L. 0.170"; "Volets: H. 0.187; L. 0.069."
2. These observations were repeated by Laborde in the 1857 edition of the volume.
3. Marquet de Vasselot 1921, I, p. 78.
4. In general, see [illegible] Corinthians (15:44–49), access to the Tree of Life (Eternal Life) is guaranteed by the death of Christ. Christ dying on the cross redeems humanity of its sins and leads people to Eternal Life. On the French sovereigns' special devotion to Mary Magdalene, first evangelist of France and patron saint of the Angevins, see Jansen 2000; Johnston 2007.
5. On the miniature, see McKentrick and Doyle 2007; on the diptych, see *Nouvelles acquisitions* 1995, no. 13.
6. Blanc 2011, cat. 8, pp. 40–41.
7. See Molinier 1903, p. 56 no. 207, pl. XII (here the piece has no frame), attributed to Nardon Pénicaud, early sixteenth century, but curiously described as "translucent enamel" ("Orfrois et fleurettes rehaussés d'émaux appliqués sur paillons. Chairs légèrement violacées. Nombreux rehauts d'or. Ciel bleu semé de nuages d'or"); each panel h. 21 cm × l. 7.5 cm; according to Molinier, originally "former les volets d'un triptyque." The piece previously in the Czartoryski collection is listed among the objects taken by the Nazis in Poland during World War II in *Division for Looted Art in the Department of Cultural Heritage Abroad and Wartime Losses*, card number 12648 (Ministry of Culture and National Heritage, Division for Looted Art).
8. *Exposition Universelle* 1867, p. 205 no. 2827; listed as owned by Countess Dzialynska, born Princess Czartoryska, which is to say Izabella Elzibieta Czartoryska, collector, painter, and wife (1857) of Count Jan Kanty Dzialynski.
9. I would like to offer my warmest thanks to Ilaria Ciseri for having found the date of the photograph for me.
10. Sale Winter Associates (Plainville, Conn., U.S.), "Continental; Art; Sculpture; Prints; Antiques: Asian; Jewelry; Silver; etc.," February 15, 2016, lot 52; "approximately" 5.25 × 4.5 inches central plaque, 5.25 × 2 inches side plaques. There are no critical indications in the auction catalogue, nor is there mention of the Bargello piece. The hypothesised chronology seems, in any case, incorrect.

RESTORATION WORK AND ANALYSIS OF MATERIALS

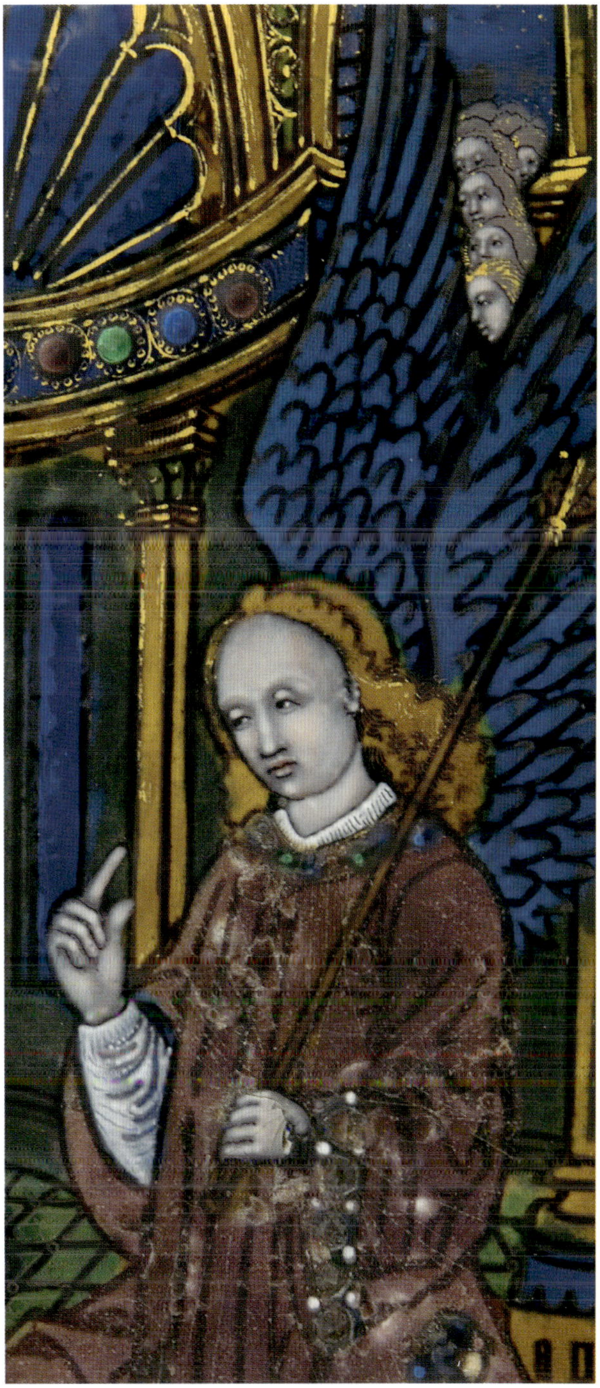

Materials and Technique

Each of the three triptychs is composed of three rectangular copper supports covered in opaque and translucent layers of enamel. The copper supports used for *Adoration, Flanked by the Virgin Annunciate and the Archangel Gabriel*, and *Man of Sorrows with the Virgin Mary and Saint John the Evangelist, Flanked by Saints Paul and Peter*, are all almost the same thickness (approximately 0.8 mm), while the support used for *Noli me tangere, Flanked by Myrrh Bearers*, is much more variable (approximately 0.5–1.2 mm), which could explain why the third piece is heavier than the others (677.8 g compared with 653.7 g for *Adoration* and 635.6 g for *Man of Sorrows*).

As is common practice in painted-enamel technique, the backs of the copper supports (figs. A, B, C) are counterenamelled to keep the plaque flat during firing.[1]

Enamelling both sides neutralises the tension generated during firing: if enamel were only applied to the front of the support, the heat would distort the plaques, and the enamel would crack during cooling. Among them, these three pieces present two different types of counterenamel: colourless with small coloured pieces in the cases of *Adoration* and *Man of Sorrows* and colourless mixed with particles of opaque white and other colours, creating an overall cerulean blue tint, in the case of *Noli me tangere*.[2]

In the nineteenth century, the plaques were set in gilded copper-alloy frames applied to backplates made of wood (common oak) in three hinged parts so that the side panels could be opened and closed. Recesses were carved into the central portions of these wooden backplates to accommodate the enamel plaques. The backplates on *Adoration* and *Noli me tangere* are, respectively, covered in red velvet and painted green with an oil-based medium, while the *Man of Sorrows* backplate is neither painted nor covered but adorned along the top with a carved motif resembling the bottom half of a rose window.

The Techniques Used to Produce the Carrand Painted Enamel Triptychs

Observing the enamelled plaques under an optical microscope reveals the technique used to create the successive layers of enamel, which was largely the same for all three triptychs: a very thin base layer of opaque white enamel was applied to the copper support, both to absorb the copper oxides that would build up on the metal during firing and to provide an optically neutral base on which to apply further colours. Before firing, a stylus was used to sketch the main outlines of the design and the figures onto this

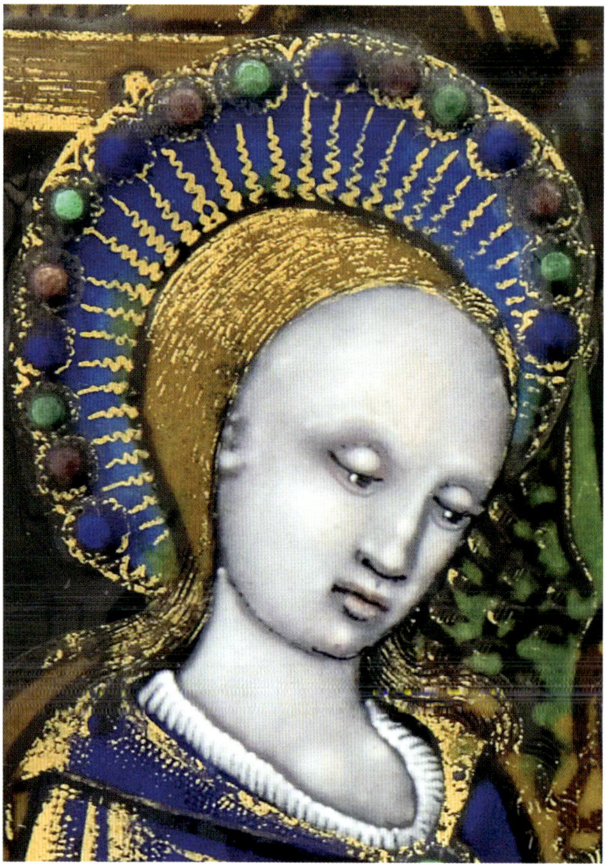

Fig. 1. The *Adoration* triptych, detail of the Virgin's face

white base layer, and the incised lines were filled with opaque red enamel.[3] After these two initial colours were fired, translucent enamels were applied to fill in the previously drawn outlines. Skin was rendered using opaque white enamel mixed with a small quantity of red to create pink flesh tones. Underneath, a thick layer of deep blue was applied, used to outline the faces and hands and occasionally exposed to create a shading effect. Touches of red were applied on top of the white enamel to emphasise certain details such as the lips (fig. 1).

A typical decorative technique in the art of painted enamel is to apply drops of enamel in relief to simulate coloured gemstones. These were used to adorn the hems of clothing, buildings, and floral elements (fig. 2), and they were raised above the flat surface of the plaque. These were created by applying a drop of enamel followed by a scrap of silver or gold leaf, which was then covered with another drop of translucent enamel. This created a mirror-like effect, reflecting light and brightening the colour of the "gem."

Sometimes the entire painted surface was covered in a

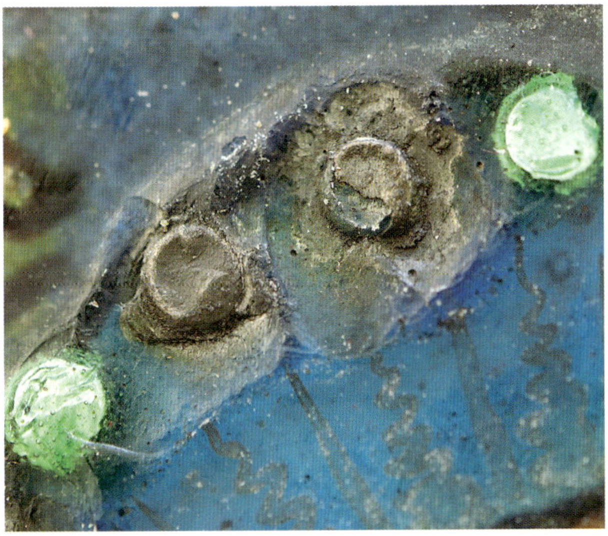

Fig. 2. The *Man of Sorrows* triptych, detail of Saint Paul's halo; in the second gemstone from the right, the silver leaf is now oxidised; in the outer two gemstones, the silver is still shiny owing to the protective enamel coating

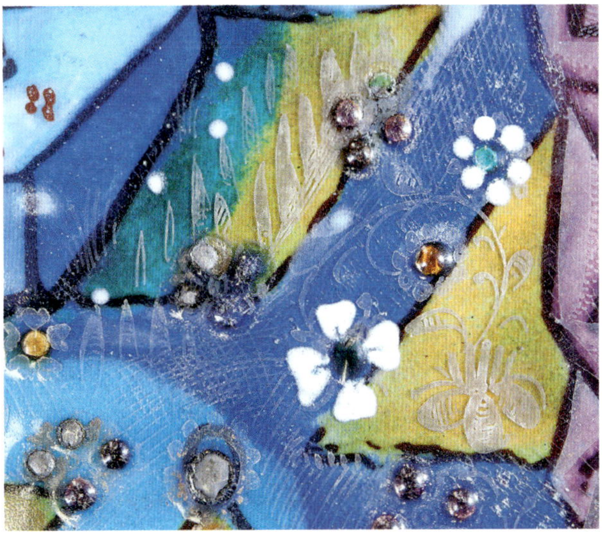

Fig. 4. The *Noli me tangere* triptych, detail observed under raking light to reveal the original gilding

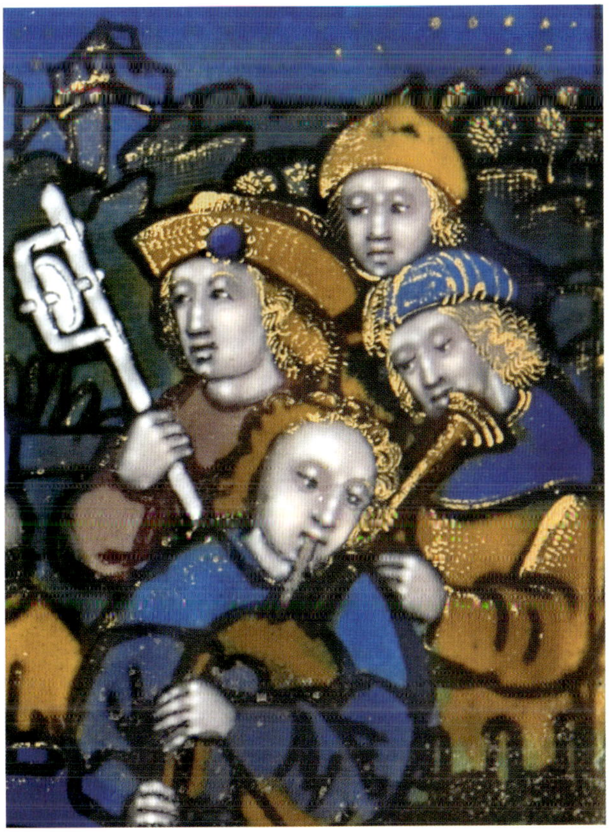

Fig. 3. The *Adoration* triptych, detail of the musicians with examples of gilding

final layer of transparent, colourless enamel called *fondant* and thereby sealed under a glossy protective coating that enhanced its brilliance.[4]

The last step in the process of creating these enamelled plaques was gilding: vegetable-based glue was applied to the areas to be gilded and then covered in gold powder or scraps of gold leaf. The firing process eliminated the glue and fixed the gold in place, permanently sealing it within the enamel as the latter softened in the heat (fig. 3). The gilding on the three triptychs is now largely abraded and worn away, to the point where it has almost completely disappeared on *Noli me tangere*, where only the imprint of the original design remains, revealed to the eye under raking light (fig. 4).

State of Conservation

The Opificio (Italy's state restoration institute) had been monitoring these three Limoges triptychs for some time, after the well-known phenomenon of leaching was detected in their enamel,[5] albeit to different degrees in each piece (fig. 5).[6] The institute had already worked on restoring *Adoration* in the 1980s and again in 2010, when a fragment of enamel came away from the left hand of the Archangel Gabriel. Products from the corrosion of the copper support were also observed, having pushed up the enamelled layer, causing it to crack. After being cleaned and consolidated, the piece was returned to the museum; the leaching phenomenon was minor at that time, visible to the naked eye as an oily film on the surface.

However, the situation worsened in recent years, almost exclusively affecting the pink-purple enamel used to depict the garments of the Virgin, Joseph, and the Angel, most likely due to a combination of effects linked to the composition of the enamel and environmental factors, which accelerated the deterioration. The reappearance of saline efflorescence from the copper support was also observed in the same piece, which weakened the enamel, causing further breakage (fig. 6). The analyses conducted by the Opificio's laboratory identified these products as copper formates derived from the interaction between the copper and formic acid emissions from the wooden backplate on which the enamelled plaques had been mounted in the nineteenth century.

To a lesser degree, problems related to leaching and the buildup of products from the corrosion of the copper support were also detected in the other two triptychs. Radical

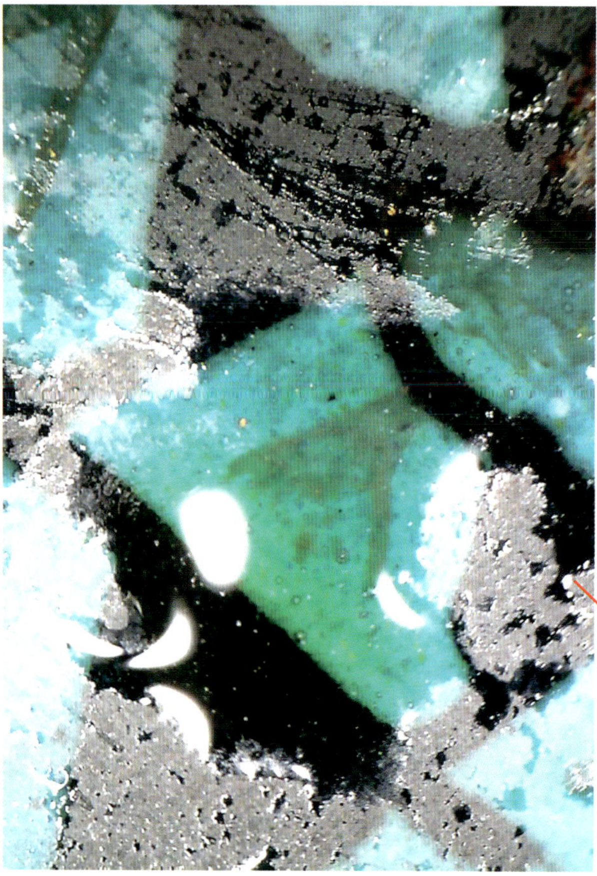

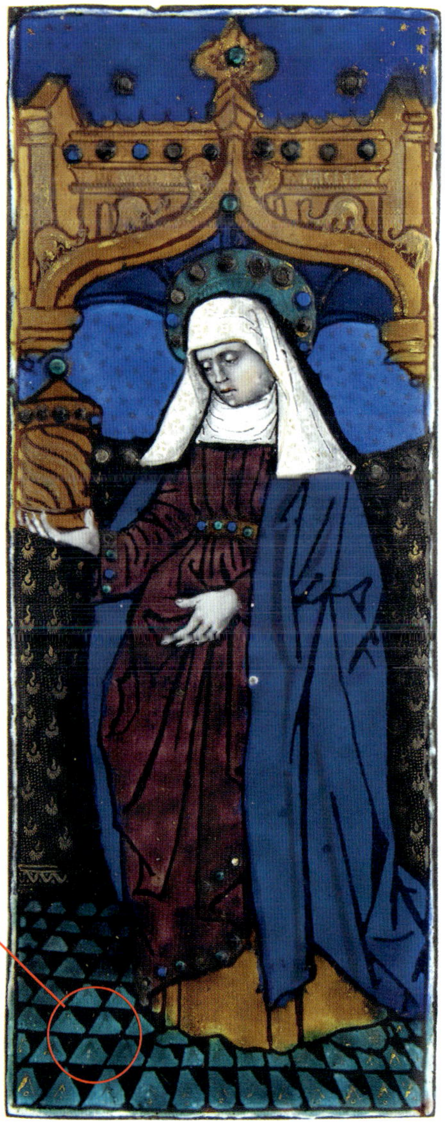

Fig. 5. The *Noli me tangere* triptych, detail with deposits of leached water-soluble components visible under the microscope

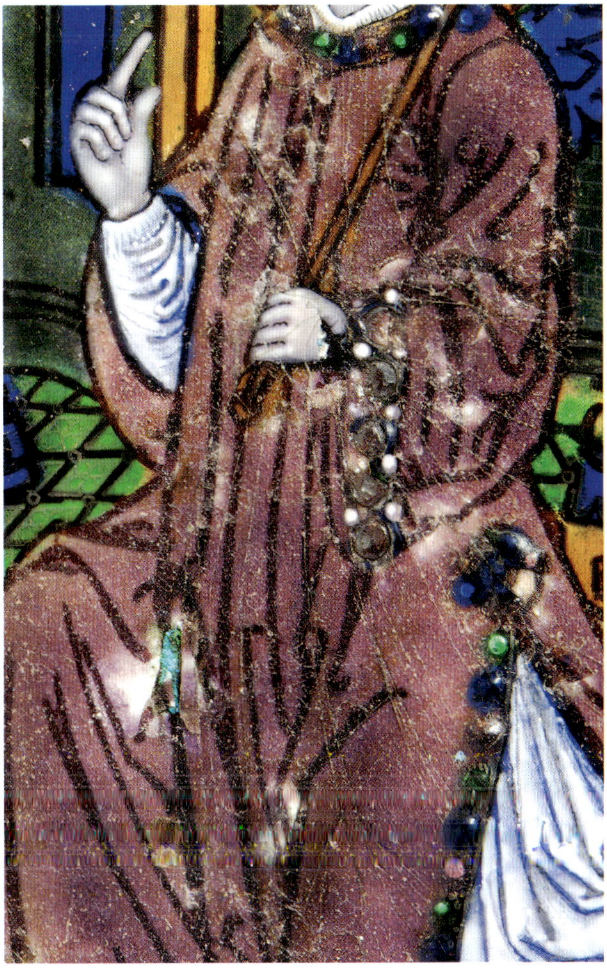

Fig. 6. The *Adoration* triptych, detail including the fragmented enamel on the Angel's robe caused by a buildup of products from the corrosion of the copper support

intervention was therefore deemed necessary to safeguard the enamels from further unstoppable deterioration.

Restoration Work

As described above, the greatest conservation challenges facing the triptychs were posed by the enamel plaques themselves; consequently, the restorers detached them from the wooden backplates by removing the gilded frames.

The plaques then underwent a preliminary degreasing by means of localised acetone swabs applied over a sheet of conservation paper. Restorers then removed the basic water-soluble components that had leached onto the surface by applying swabs of agar made with deionised water, once again over conservation paper. The enamels were dried using swabs of ethyl alcohol and acetone.

The products of copper corrosion were removed mechanically under an optical microscope by means of scalpels, needle tips, and other metal probes. Work on the *Adoration* triptych had already taken place in 2010, when the left hand of the Angel was cleaned to remove the salts produced by the deterioration process, and fragments of detached enamel were secured by infiltrating a suitable adhesive. This operation was repeated in the recent intervention, this time on a fragment of the Angel's robe, where the enamel had been forced upward and fractured by the corrosion products that had built up between the enamel and the copper support (fig. 7).

The wooden backplates were removed and would be omitted from the new mounts. However, the gilded frames were to be retained and were therefore cleaned using organic solvents. Restorers removed the products of

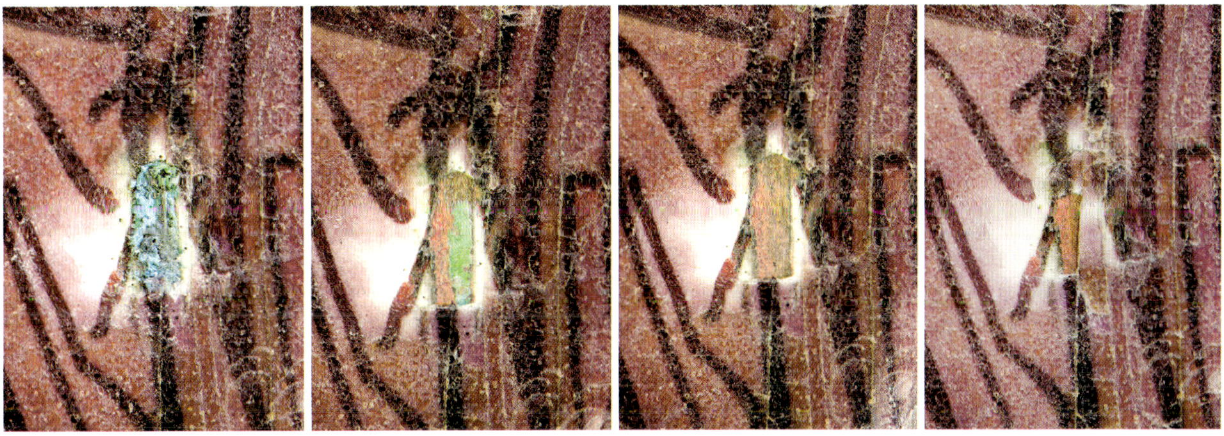

Fig. 7. The *Adoration* triptych, detail of the Angel's robe, showing the removal of copper corrosion products and subsequent consolidation of the detached fragment of translucent enamel

the deterioration of the metal alloy by mechanical means and with localised swabs of a suitable chelating solution.

The Need for a New Environment

To prevent the disintegration of the enamel caused by leaching, the plaques had to be sealed within a protected and microclimatically stable environment that kept relative humidity levels low. To eliminate the possibility of developing new copper formates, it was decided to omit the wooden backplates, which would have continued to emit formic acid fumes. Nowadays, several alternative mounting materials are available, designed to remain chemically inert and stable over time. The material chosen was a closed-cell expanded polyethylene product called Plastazote®, which had already been used at the Bargello Museum to mount Andrea Pucci Sardi da Empoli's *Fregio*, an enamel frieze. Plastazote®, which has also been tested by the Opificio's laboratory, can be cut and shaped with great precision. The new mounts were manufactured by a specialist company,[7] and the enamel plaques and gilded frames were remounted once restoration was complete.

For increased stability, it was decided to mount each triptych on a single piece of Plastazote® rather than reproduce the original three-panel structure, which the tripartite frames nevertheless continued to suggest. The new mounts were cut and shaped using 3D scanning techniques, with central recesses cut out to securely accommodate the three plaques. From among the various types of Plastazote® available, the one selected was of the correct thickness to receive the original nails (replicating soft wood in this respect) so that the gilded frames could be safely refitted.

Paolo Belluzzo, Riccardo Gennaioli & Cinzia Ortolani

---

1. See, for example, Speel 1998, pp. 33–34; Arminjon and Bilimoff 1998, p. 213 note 5; Biron 2015, pp. 332–334.
2. Counterenamel frequently contains various colours because it was traditionally made using the recycled leftovers from other enamels produced in the workshops. However, it has been noted that counterenamel composition points to the development of a certain coherent trend in Limoges, suggesting that this phase came to mean more than just an opportunity to recycle waste material. See Biron 2015, p. 333.
3. On different uses of colour in the base layer of painted enamels, see Arminjon and Bilimoff 1998, pp. 212–213 notes 2–4.
4. This finishing coat of colourless enamel (*émail peint sous fondant*) is rarely encountered on painted enamels, partly because it is difficult to identify; however, it has demonstrated its protective function over time, especially when applied to frequently handled objects such as cases, tobacco tins, and clocks. See, for example, Arminjon and Bilimoff 1998, p. 220 and note 8. Nevertheless, certain texts suggest it was applied to objects that were not strictly intended for use: Meyer 1895, pp. 23, 25; Bourdery 1888, pp. 13, 16, 19.
5. On the phenomenon of leaching from enamel, see the essay by Cagnini et al. elsewhere in this volume.
6. This form of deterioration, known commonly as leaching, is a chemical process linked to the presence of water, which causes water- soluble substances within the enamel to leach out and form deposits.
7. Isopad, Sogimi Group, Prato (PO).

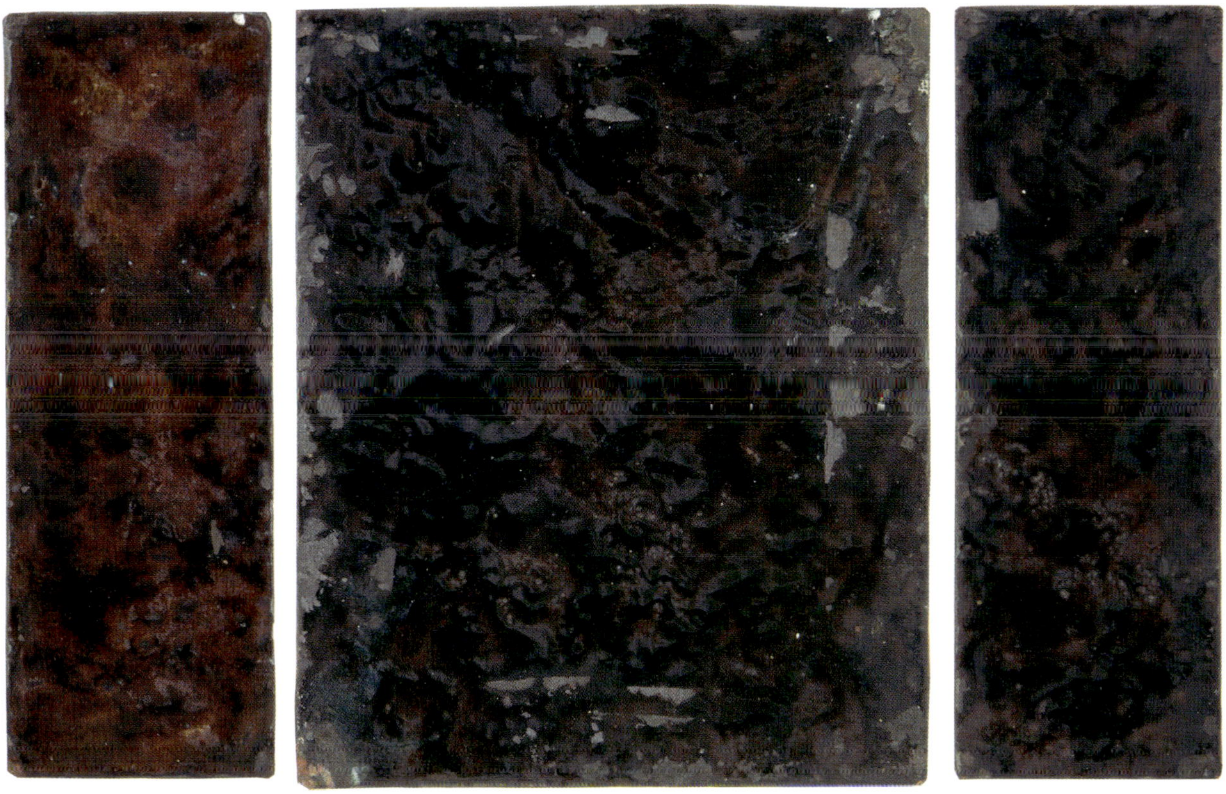

Fig. A. The *Man of Sorrows* triptych, back side

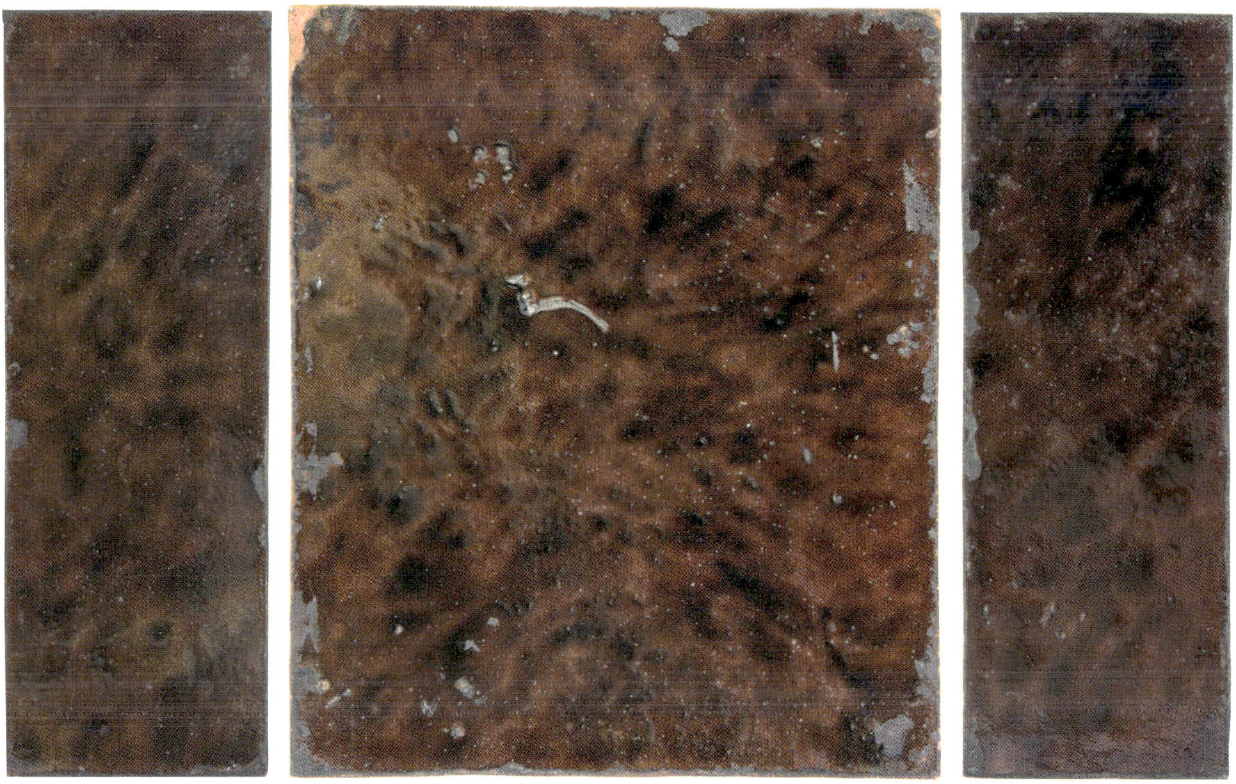

Fig. B. The *Adoration* triptych, back side

Fig. C. The *Noli me tangere* triptych, back side

Scientific Studies to Identify Constituent Materials and Manifestations of Deterioration

In response to alarming signs of deterioration, such as salt efflorescences (sulfates and formates essentially, identified by infrared spectroscopy), condensation, and fragmentation of enamel (fig. 1) on the surfaces of the *Adoration* and *Noli me tangere* triptychs, investigations were made into the causes of the damage with a view to impeding its progress.

Two micro-fragments of deteriorated purple enamel that had come away from the surface of *Adoration* and could not be reattached were analysed using a scanning electron microscope with a microprobe (SEM-EDS). The SEM image (fig. 2) of their cross sections clearly shows two zones distinguished by two different shades of gray. The central part has a sodium content of around 16% and a potassium content of around 8%, while the surface part, where large fractures are observed, contains markedly lower concentrations of these elements (sodium is reduced to 2% and potassium to around 4%). This deterioration is closely linked not only to the composition of the enamel but also to the relative humidity of the environment: the surface of the enamel absorbs water from the air, and when the relative humidity exceeds 43–44%, condensation and even water droplets can form on the surface (as observed in these two pieces). This triggers a deterioration process called leaching, whereby hydrogen ions in the water are exchanged for sodium and potassium ions in the glass matrix. The latter are extracted from the glass and react on the surface with substances present in the environment (carbon dioxide, sulfur oxides, organic acids, etc.), which sometimes derive from surrounding materials, such as wood or cloth in the display case. These reactions form salts (carbonates, sulfates, acetates, formates, etc.), which are either dissolved in the surface water or present in crystalline form when the humidity is reduced. This thin layer of alkaline components can cause mechanical tensions in the structure of the enamel, which, due to the difference in its physical characteristics compared to non-deteriorated sections, may then suffer fractures and material losses. The phenomenon is accelerated by the repeated solubilisation and precipitation of the salts, which can migrate deeper into the enamel through small fractures or pores, inducing further fractures that can even cause fragments of unaltered enamel to detach. Therefore, it is clearly important to maintain an extremely controlled microclimate, with a low and constant humidity rate, in

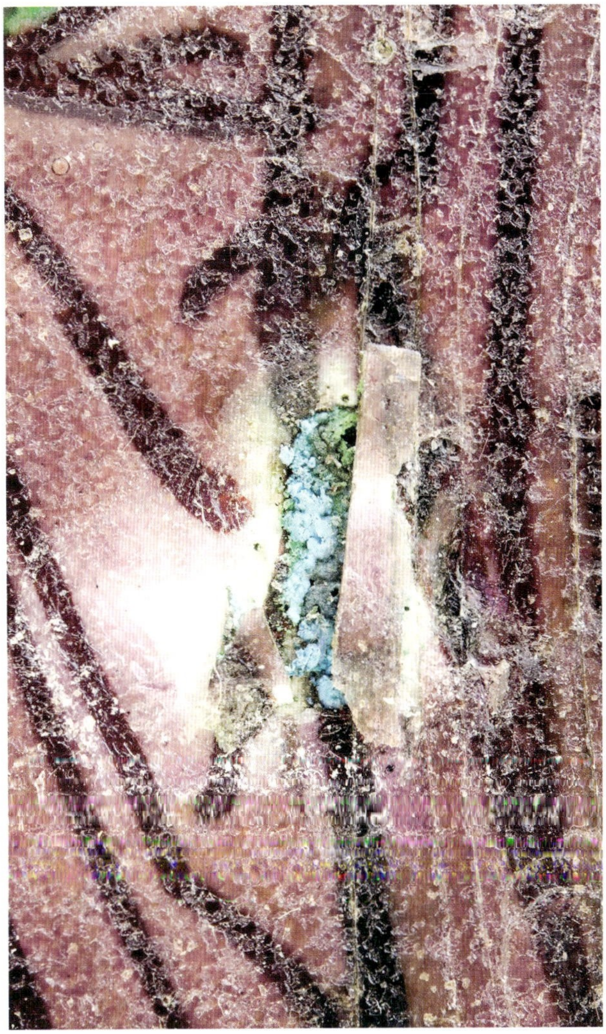

Fig. 1. Surface of the enamel on the *Noli me tangere* triptych showing blue-coloured salt efflorescence and deterioration of the purple enamel with detachment of microfragments

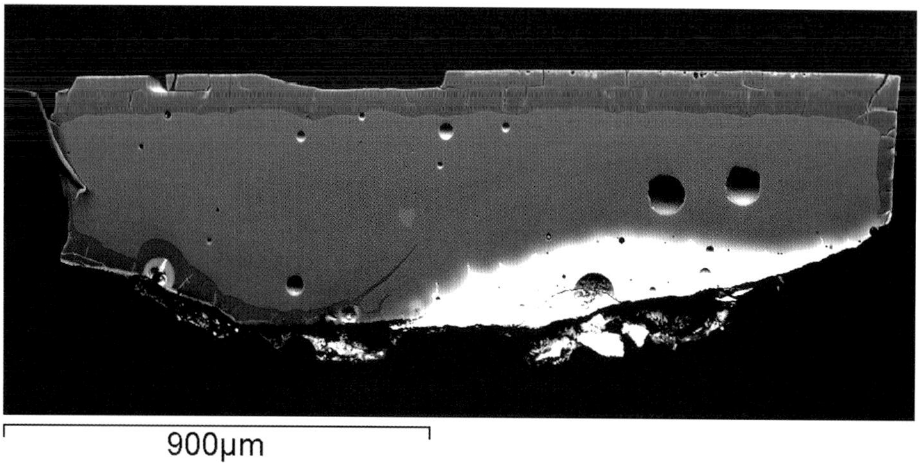

Fig. 2. SEM-EDS image of a fragment of purple enamel from *Adoration* in cross section, revealing the presence of areas of different shades of gray within the glass matrix, indicative of compositional differences

a display case free from potentially damaging materials.

Besides being an essential step in preserving the artefact, the restoration work is also an invaluable opportunity to carry out archaeometric studies on the piece itself. For example, the SEM-EDS analysis of the two fragments revealed that the translucent enamel in the sample was produced using purified plant ash (indicated by calcium content of around 4% and very low concentrations of magnesium and phosphorus, at around 0.6% and 0.1%, respectively) and a source of silicon, which was also purified (indicated by low aluminum content of around 0.5%). Moreover, a total absence of lead was observed. On the other hand, the small portions of opaque white enamel, seen in in the cross section (fig. 2) section next to the purple enamel, are characterised by a matrix rich in lead, in which tin acts as an opacifying agent in the form of cassiterite. Further information can be obtained in a non-invasive way by using portable X-ray fluorescence (pXRF)[1] to identify the elements involved in colouring the enamel (as shown in the accompanying table).

Enamel colour	Colouring elements
Blue and light blue (turquoise in *Noli me tangere* and *Man of Sorrows*)	Cobalt
Brown (in *Noli me tangere* and *Adoration*)	Iron and manganese
Yellow (in *Adoration*)	Iron
Purple	Manganese
Gilded areas	Gold
Green	Copper and iron
White (skin tone)	Lead and tin

Additional data can be derived from the study of lead signal ratios in pXRF spectra recorded on opaque white areas and on areas of other colours; in fact, those ratios show that the glass constituting the translucent enamel is essentially lead-free and that the lead signal present in these spectra comes from underlying layers of opaque enamel.

The metal support could only be analysed in the *Man of Sorrows* triptych (at the one point where it was free from enamel). An extremely high copper signal was detected along with very low signals for iron, nickel, zinc, lead, arsenic, antimony, and tin. Although the literature does not report many analyses of such supports, published data essentially show the same types of trace elements.[2]

The thickness of the enamel on the three artefacts was ascertained by measuring Eddy Currents. The average thickness of the glass on the front is approximately 400–500 microns, while it is thinner on the back, at approximately 200–300 microns.

Identifying the period of production is a complex matter. The glass on the back of all three triptychs, in the areas studied, appears to be essentially lead-free and could therefore be dated to the sixteenth century. Indeed, the literature reports that more modern enamels[3] are all rich in lead, even if this conclusion is based on a limited number of objects.

The presence of cobalt accessory elements in blue enamel, for example, can generally be used to define the production period more precisely, since the mines from which this element was extracted were rare and active in a fairly distinct historical period, and the extracted mineral has a generally indicative compositional pattern. In this case, a coherent pattern is observed between high signals of cobalt, nickel, and arsenic, where present, while correlations of cobalt with zinc are not observed. These data suggest that the enamel used in *Adoration* was produced in the sixteenth century, probably after 1520–1530, while the enamel in *Man of Sorrows* and *Noli me tangere*, lacking in arsenic, would appear to date from an earlier period. The turquoise enamel used in *Noli me tangere* and in *Man of Sorrows* was derived, yet again, from cobalt, a technique that was also more common in the period before 1520–1530. Variation in the source of the cobalt mineral is observed in painted enamels as well as other types of objects, such as the "Venetian" enamels on copper and the Della Robbia glazed ceramics.[4] However, it must be borne in mind that the boundaries between periods in which the various minerals were used are obviously not clear-cut, and certain pieces do not correspond with this model.

The challenge of correctly identifying the production period is particularly marked in the case of *Adoration*. One of the most characteristic phenomena observed in these types of works, and cited in the literature, concerns the enamel on pieces produced between 1480 and 1530: enamel in blue and varying shades of purple applied to specific areas of the designs frequently suffers high levels of deterioration, while other colours on the same pieces, or even the same colour but in different parts of the designs, are excellently preserved. The purple garments in *Adoration* are a particularly clear example of this. This tendency to deteriorate is closely linked to a high concentration of alkaline ions (sodium and potassium) and a lower concentration of ions such as aluminium and calcium (known for their stabilising capacity) due to the purification of the silicon sources and the ash, as revealed by the quantitative analysis of enamel fragments. Using purer sources and adding higher concentrations of potassium resulted in a brighter enamel, which, one can assume, was applied to the most precious parts of the piece, such as the garments of the Madonna or the saints, to emphasise the importance of the figures. Other elements such as buildings, which had no specific aesthetic requirements to meet, were probably depicted using duller but much more stable enamels. Hence the coexistence of deteriorated parts and preserved parts, even in the same colour, on the same piece. No such deterioration is observed in purple enamel from later periods, generally after 1530, suggesting a—probably deliberate—change in composition which reduced the problem.

However, this interpretation clearly precludes the dating of *Adoration* to after 1530 (based on the presence of cobalt accessory elements in the blue enamel), thereby highlighting the need for more detailed research into the materials and dating of such works.

Andrea Cagnini, Monica Galeotti,
Simone Porcinai & Alessandra Santagostino Barbone

1. Syta et al. 2018; Van der Linden et al. 2010; Röhrs and Stege 2004.
2. Biron 2015, pp. 315–371.
3. Biron 2015, pp. 315–371.
4. Biron 2015, pp. 315–371; Verità et al. 2018; Zucchiatti et al. 2006.

BIBLIOGRAPHY

Adhémar 1975 = Adhémar, Jean. "Une galerie de portraits italiens à Amboise en 1500." *Gazette des Beaux-Arts* 86, no. 1281 (1957): 99–104.

Aldovini 2014 = Aldovini, Laura. "La stampa con il 'Cristo portacroce' e la trasmissione dei modelli nell'arte lombarda della fine del XV e inizi del XVI secolo." In *L'Andata al Calvario di Marco Palmezzano: Restauri, ricerche, interpretazioni*, conference proceedings (Lovere, Accademia Tadini, 2012), edited by Vincenzo Gheroldi, pp. 87–96. Lovere: Accademia di Belle Arti Tadini, 2014.

Ardant 1828 = Ardant, Maurice. "Des émaux de Limoges." *Bulletin de la Société Royale d'Agricolture, des Sciences et Arts de Limoges* 8, no. 3 (1828): 89–102.

Ardant 1842 = Ardant, Maurice. *Notice Historique sur les émaux, les* émailleurs, *leurs divers ouvrages, et les procédés de fabrication en usage a Limoges*. Limoges: Chapouland Frères, 1842.

Ardant 1854 = Ardant, Maurice. "Nouvelles recherches sur les émailleurs limousins." *Bulletin de la Société Archéologique et Historique du Limousin* 5 (1854): 105–111.

Ardant [1844] 1855 = Ardant, Maurice. *Émailleurs et émaillerie de Limoges* [1844]. Isle: Typographie Martial Ardant Fréres, 1855.

Ardant 1857 = Ardant, Maurice. "Émailleurs limousins." *Bulletin de la Societè Archèologique et Historique du Limousin* 7 (1857): 61–68.

Ardant 1858 = Ardant, Maurice. "Émailleurs Limousins: Les Pénicaud." *Bulletin de la Société Archéologique et Historique du Limousin* 8 (1858): 5–32.

Arminjon and Bilimoff 1998 = Arminjon, Catherine, and Michèle Bilimoff. *L'art du métal: Vocabulaire technique*. Paris: Imprimerie Nationale, 1998.

Arquié-Bruley 1989 = Arquié-Bruley, Françoise. "Acquisitions Carrand à l'Hôtel Drouot, 1835–1885." In *Arti del Medio Evo e del Rinascimento* 1989, pp. 183–208.

Arquié-Bruley 1990 = Arquié-Bruley, Françoise. "Debruge-Duménil (1788–1838) et sa collection d'objets d'art." *Annali della Scuola Normale Superiore di Pisa: Classe di Lettere e Filosofia* s. III, 20, no. 1 (1990): 211–248.

Arquié-Bruley 1998 = Arquié-Bruley, Françoise. "Émaux limousins et collectionneurs au début du XIXe siècle." In *L'oeuvre de Limoges: Art et histoire au temps des Plantagenêts*, conference proceedings (Partis, Musée du Louvre, 1995), edited by Danielle Gaborit-Chopin and Élisabeth Taburet-Delahaye, 19–45. Paris: La Documentation Française, 1998.

Arti del Medio Evo e del Rinascimento 1989 = *Arti del Medio Evo e del Rinascimento: Omaggio ai Carrand 1889–1989*, catalogue of the exhibition (Florence, Museo Nazionale del Bargello, 1989), edited by Giovanna Gaeta Bertelà and Beatrice Paolozzi Strozzi. Florence: SPES, 1989.

Bache Collection 1943 = *The Bache Collection: A Loan Exhibition at the Metropolitan Museum of Art*, catalogue of the exhibition (New York, Metropolitan Museum of Art, June 16–September 30, 1943), edited by Jules Semon Bache. New York: William Bradford, 1943.

Baert 2012 = Baert, Barbara. "The Gaze in the Garden: Mary Magdalene in *Noli me tangere*." In *Mary Magdalene: Iconographic Studies from the Middle Ages to the Baroque*, edited by Michelle A. Erhardt and Amy M. Morris, 189–222. Leiden: Brill, 2012.

Bailey and Hodgkins 2014 = Bailey, Gregory H., and Robyn E. Hodgkins. "Silver Surface Decoration on Limoges Painted Enamel." *Metropolitan Museum Studies in Art, Science and Technology* 2 (2014): 157–165.

Balzac 1855 = Balzac, Honoré de. *Les contes drolatiques*. Paris: Société Génerale de Librairie, 1855.

Baratte 1993 = Baratte, Sophie. *Léonard Limosin au Musée du Louvre*. Paris: Réunion des Musées Nationaux, 1993.

Baratte 2000 = Baratte, Sophie. *Musée du Louvre, Départment des objets d'art: Les émaux peints du Limoges—Catalogue*. Paris: Réunion des Musées Nationaux, 2000.

Béguin 1985 = Béguin, Sylvie. *Andrea Solario en France*. Paris: Réunion des Musées Nationaux, 1985

Belli Barsali 1966 = Belli Barsali, Isa. *Lo smalto in Europa*. Milan: Fabbri, 1966.

Bentley-Cranach 1988 = Bentley-Cranach, Dana. "A Sixteenth-Century Patron of the Arts, Florimond Robertet, Baron d'Alluye and His 'Vierge Ouvrante.'" *Bibliothéque d'Humanisme et Renaissance* 50 (1988): 317–333.

Beyssi-Cassan 2006 = Beyssi-Cassan, Maryvonne. *Le métier d'émailleur à Limoges, XVIe–XVIIe siècle*. Limoges: PULIM, 2006.

Biron 1999 = Biron, Isabelle. "Study of XVth and XVIth Century Painted Enamels throught Scientific Analysis: Causes of Glass Deterioration." *Berliner Beiträge zur Archäimetrie* 16 (1999): 129–135.

Biron 2015 = Biron, Isabelle. *Émaux sur métal du IXe au XIXe siècle: Histoire, technique et matériaux*. Dijon: Faton, 2015.

Blair and Campbell 2008 = Blair, Claude, and Marian Campbell. *Louis Marcy: Oggetti d'arte della Galleria Parmeggiani di Reggio Emilia*. Turin: Allemandi, 2008.

Blanc 2011 = Blanc, Monique. *Émaux peints de Limoges, XVe–XVIIIe siècle: La collection du Musée des Arts Décoratifs*. Paris: Les Arts Décoratifs, 2011.

Blunt [1953] 1980 = Blunt, Anthony. *Art and Architecture in France from 1500 to 1700* [1953]. London: Penguin, 1980.

Bourdery 1888 = Bourdery, Louis. *Exposition rétrospective de Limoges en 1886: Les émaux peints*. Limoges: Imprimerie et Librairie Limousine V. H. Ducourtieux, 1888.

Bourdery 1890 = Bourdery, Louis. *Notice sommaire sur les émaux peints de Limoges*. Limoges: Imprimerie et Librairie Limousine V. H. Ducourtieux, 1890.

Bourdery and Lachenaud 1889 = Bourdery, Louis, and Émile Lachenaud. *Essai d'inventaire général historique et critique de l'oeuvre des anciens peintres émailleurs de Limoges*. Limoges: Imprimerie et Librairie Limousine V. H. Ducourtieux, 1889.

Bourdery and Lachenaud 1897 = Bourdery, Louis, and Émile Lachenaud. *L'oeuvre des peintres émailleurs de Limoges: Léonard Limosin, peintre de portraits, d'après les catalogues des ventes, de musées et d'expositons, et les auteurs qui se sont occupés de ces* émaux. Paris: L.-H. May, 1897.

Brioist 2020 = Brioist, Pascal. "Shaping Romorantin Anew in 1517–1518: Leonardo's Projects in Context." In *L'ultimo Leonardo, 1510–1519: Leonardo tra Milano, Roma e Amboise: Committenze, progetti, studi fra arte, architettura e scienza*, conference proceedings (Milan, Palazzo Reale, 2019), edited by Pietro C. Marani, 209–219. Busto Arsizio: Nomos, 2020.

Brown 1987 = Brown, David Alan. *Andrea Solario*. Milan: Electa, 1987.

Burger 1930 = Burger, Willy. *Abendländische Schmelzarbeiten*. Berlin: Richard Carl Schmidt, 1930.

Carocci 1892 = Carocci, Guido . "Alcuni bronzi della raccolta Carrand nel Museo Nazionale di Firenze." *Arte italiana decorativa e industriale* 2, no. 2 (1892): 14–15.

Carosselli 1993 = Carosselli, Susan L. *The Painted Enamels of Limoges: A Catalogue of the Collection of the Los Angeles County Museum of Art*. Los Angeles: Los Angeles Museum of Art, 1993.

Catalogue 1843 = *Catalogue de la collection formée par M. Didier Petit, à Lyon . . .* Paris: Dentu, 1843.

Catalogue 1849 = *Catalogue des objets d'art qui composent la collection Debruge-Duménil*. Paris: Roussels, 1849.

Catalogue 1863 = *Catalogue of the Special Exhibition of Works of Art of the Mediaeval, Renaissance, and More Recent Periods, on Loan at the South Kensington Museum, June 1862*, edited by J. C. Robinson. London: Spottiswoode, 1863.

Catalogue 1875 = *Catalogue of the Special Loan Exhibition of Enamels on Metal Held at the South Kensington Museum in 1874*, preface by John Hungerford Pollen. London: Chiswick, 1875.

Chastel 1974 = Chastel, André. "Signature et Signe." *Revue de l'art* 26 (1974): 8–14.

Chastel 1994 = Chastel, André. *L'art français: Temps modernes 1430–1620*. Paris: Flammarion, 1994.

Chevallier 1991 = Chevallier, Bernard. "Les émaux de Sèvres." *L'Estampille-L'Object d'Art*, 245 (1991): 44–57.

Collection Spitzer 1890–1891 = *La collection Spitzer: Antiquité, Moyen Âge, Renaissance*, 2 vols. Mâcon: Protat Frères, 1890–1891.

Cordera 2008 = Cordera, Paola. *Ottocento italiano e smalti di Limoges: La produzione dell'atelier Pénicaud tra revival, collezionismo e arti industriali*. [Vicchio]: LoGisma, 2008.

Cyril Humphris Collection 1995 = *The Cyril Humphris Collection of European Sculptures and Works of Art*, auction catalogue (New York, Sotheby's, January 11, 1995), 2 vols. New York: Sotheby's, 1995.

D'Amato 2022 = D'Amato, Martina A. "*Il passa les Alpes avec ses trésors*: Louis Carrand and Florence." In *Florence ville d'art et les Français: La création d'un mythe*, conference proceedings (Florence, Villa Finlay, Centre André Chastel, 2019), edited by Anne Lepoittevin, Emmanuel Lurin, and Alain Mérot. Rome: Campisano, 2022, pp. 153-168.

Darcel 1861 = Darcel, Alfred. "La collection Soltykoff." *Gazette des Beaux-Arts* 10, no. 55 (1861): 212–226.

Darcel 1862 = Darcel, Alfred. "Les arts industriels à l'Exposition de Londres: L'émaillerie, les bronzes et la Fonte de fer." *Gazette des Beaux-Arts* 13, no. 73 (1862): 538–555.

Darcel 1863 = Darcel, Alfred. "Exposition des Beaux-Arts appliqués à l'industrie." *Gazette des Beaux-Arts* 15, no. 5 (1863): 481–486.

Darcel 1867 = Darcel, Alfred. *Notice des émaux et de l'orfèvrerie*. Paris: Charles de Morgues Frères, 1867.

Dehan 2021 = Dehan, Maxime. *La vie romanesque de Didier Petit de Meurville (1793–1873)*, part 2, https://lyonnais.hypotheses.org/6020.

Distelberger 2000 = Distelberger, Rudolf. "Les moulages en plâtre et modèles de bijoux de l'atelier du restaurateur Alfred André (1839–1919)." In *Joyaux Renaissance une splendeur retrouvée*, edited by Jacques Kugel. Paris: Kugel, 2000, n. p.

Distelberger et al.1993 = Distelberger, Rudolf, Alison Luchs, Philippe Verdier, and Timothy Wilson. *The Collections of the National Gallery of Art Systematic Catalogue: Western Decorative Art, Part I, Medieval, Renaissance and Historicizing Styles Including Metalwork, Enamels and Ceramics*. Washington, D.C.: National Gallery of Art, 1993.

Drayman-Weisser 2003 = Drayman-Weisser, Terry. "The Early Painted Enamels of Limoges in the Walters Art Museum: Historical Context and Observations on Past Treatments." *Journal of the American Institute for Conservations* 42, no. 2 (2003): 279–312.

Du Sommerard 1838–1843 = Du Sommerard, Alexandre. *Les art de Moyen Âge, en ce qui concerne principalement le Palais Romain de Paris, l'Hôtel de Cluny issu de ses ruines et les objets d'art de la collection classée dans cet hôtel*, 4 vols. Paris: A l'Hôtel de Cluny et Chez Techener, 1838–1843.

Dussieux 1841 = Dussieux, Louis. *Recherches sur l'histoire de la peinture sur émail dans les temps anciens et modernes, et spécialement en France*. Paris: Leleux, 1841.

Esposizione 1887 = *Esposizione donatelliana nel R. Museo Nazionale in Firenze*. Florence: Fratelli Bencini, 1887.

Eudel 1883 = Eudel, Paul. *L'Hôtel Drouot et la curiosité en 1882*, preface by Armand Silvestre. Paris: G. Charpentier, 1883.

Eudel 1884 = Eudel, Paul. *Le truquage: Les contrefaçons devoilées*. Paris: E. Dentu, 1884.

Evans 1987 = Evans, Mark L. "New Light on the 'Sforziada' Frontespieces of Giovan Pietro Birago." *British Library Journal* 13, no. 2 (1987): 232–247.

Exposition Universelle 1867 = *Exposition Universelle de 1867 à Paris: Catalogue général publié par la commission impériale: Histoire du travail et monuments historiques*. Paris/London: E. Dentu–J. M. Johnson, 1867.

Fagnart 2009 = Fagnart, Laure. *Léonard de Vinci en France: Collections et collectionneurs (XVIe–XVIIe siècle)*. Rome: L'Erma di Bretschneider, 2009

Fagnart and Miesse 2015 = Fagnart, Laure, and Hélène Miesse. "Perché havemo bisogno ancora de maestro Leonardo. Léonard de Vinci au service de Charles II Chaumont d'Amboise." *Raccolta Vinciana* 36 (2015): 47–76.

Falize 1893 = Falize, Lucien. "Claudius Popelin et la renaissance des émaux peints." *Gazette des Beaux-Arts* 35, no. 9 (1893): 418–435, 508–512; no. 10 (1893): 60–76, 426–437, 478–489.

Falize 1894 = Falize, Lucien. "Claudius Popelin et la renaissance des émaux peints (fin)." *Gazette des Beaux-Arts* 36, no. 9 (1894): 130–148.

Ferrari 2020 = Ferrari, Simone. *Dürer e Leonardo: Il paragone delle arti a nord e a sud delle Alpi*. Genoa: Genoa University Press, 2020.

Ferrer 2006 = Jean-Marc Ferrer. "La redécouverte de l'émail à Limoges au XXe siècle: l'Exposition du Centre de la France en 1858, une exibition à reconsidérer." In *Les émaux peints limousins: Au coeur des arts décoratifs de la Renaissance*, conference proceedings (Limoges, 2004), edited by Jean Tricard, Philippe Grandcoing, and Robert Chanaud, 211– 237. Limoges: PULIM, 2006.

Fiorio 1997 = Fiorio, Maria Teresa. "Leonardo, Boltraffio e Jean Perréal." *Raccolta Vinciana* 27 (1997): 325–355.

Firenze e contorni 1891 = *Firenze e contorni: Catalogo N. 1. riproduzioni fotografiche pubblicate per cura dei Fratelli Alinari fotografi-editori*. Florence: Fratelli Alinari, 1891.

Florence 1895 = *Florence: Collection Carrand au Bargello*. Rome: G. Sangiorgi, 1895.

Fontaine 1932 = Fontaine, G. "Pénicaud." In *Allgemeines Lexicon der Bildenden Künstler von der Antike bis zur Gegemwart* 26, Ulrich Thieme and Felix Becker, 370–380. Leipzig: E. A. Seeman, 1932.

Franks 1858–1859 = Franks, Augustus Wollaston. "From A. W. Franks Esq. Director." *Proceeding of the Society of Antiquaries of London* 4 (1858–1859): 248–249.

Franzon 2004 = Franzon, Maria. "An Approach to Authenticity Problems of Painted Limoges Enamels." *Neue Forschungen zum Maleremail aus Limoges* (2004): 108–116.

Gaborit-Chopin 2018 = Gaborit-Chopin, Danielle. "I Carrand padre e figlio e gli avori del Museo Nazionale del Bargello." In *Gli avori del Museo Nazionale del Bargello*, edited by Ilaria Ciseri, 22–26. Milan: Officina Libraria, 2018.

Galli 2018 = Galli, Lavinia M. "Il collezionismo dei rami smaltati detti veneziani e la recezione della storiografia francese in Italia nel XIX secolo." In *I rami smaltati detti veneziani del Rinascimento italiano / Les cuivres émaillés dits vénitiens de la Renaissance italienne*, conference proceedings (Venice, Fondazione Giorgio Cini, 2014), edited by Françoise Barbe, Isabelle Biron, Letizia Caselli, and Marie-Elsa Dantan, 105–119. Cinisello Balsamo: Silvana, 2018.

Garmier 1980 = Garmier, Jean-François. "Le goût du Moyen Âge chez les collectionneurs lyonnais du XIXe siècle." *Revue de l'art* 47 (1980): 53–64.

Gauthier 1987 = Gauthier, Marie-Madeleine. *Émaux méridionaux: Catalogue international de l'oeuvre de Limoges, I, L'époque romane*. Paris: Centre National de la Recherche Scientifique, 1987.

Gautier 1852 = Gautier, Théophile. *Émaux et camées*. Paris: E. Didier, 1852.

Georges Ier d'Amboise 2013 = *Georges Ier d'Amboise, 1460–1510: Une figure plurielle de la Renaissance*, conference proceedings (Liège, 2010), edited by Jonathan Dumont and Laure Fagnart. Rennes: Presses Universitaires de Rennes, 2013.

Gerspach 1904 = Gerspach, Eduard. "La Collection Carrand au Musée National de Florence." *Les Arts* 3, no. 31 (1904): 2–32.

I Carrand e il collezionismo 1989 = *I Carrand e il collezionismo francese, 1820–1888*, catalogue of the exhibition (Florence, Museo Nazionale del Bargello, 1989). Florence: Museo Nazionale del Bargello, 1989.

Jansen 2000 = Jansen, Katherine Ludwig. *The Making of the Magdalen: Preaching and Popular Devotion in the Later Middle Ages*. Princeton: Princeton University Press, 2000.

Johnston 2007 = Johnston, Barbara J. "Sacred Kingship and Royal Patronage in the *Vie de la Magdalene*: Pilgrimage, Politics, Passion Plays and the Life of Louise of Savoy." PhD dissertation, Florida State University, 2007.

Labarte 1847 = Labarte, Jules. *Description des objets d'art qui composent la collection Debruge-Duménil, précédée d'une introduction historique*. Paris: Victor Didron, 1874.

Labarte 1856 = Labarte, Jules. *Recherches sur la peinture en émail dans l'Antiquité et au Moyen Âge*. Paris: Victor Didron, 1856.

Labarte 1865–1866 = Labarte, Jules. *Histoire des arts industriel au Moyen Âge et à l'époque de la Renaissance*, 2 vols. Paris: A. Morel, 1865–1866.

Labarte 1875 = Labarte, Jules. *Histoire des arts industriel au Moyen Âge et à l'époque de la Reinassance*, XIII. Paris: A. Morel, 1875.

Laborde 1852 = Laborde, Léon de. *Notice des émaux exposés dans les galeries du Musée du Louvre*, I: *Histoire et descriptions*. Paris: Vinchon, 1852.

Laborde 1853 = Laborde, Léon de. *Notice des émaux, bijoux et objets divers exposés dans les galeries du Musée du Louvre*, I: *Histoire et descriptions*. Paris: Vinchon, 1853.

Laborde 1857 = Laborde, Léon de. *Notice des émaux, bijoux et objects divers exposés dans les galeries du Musée du Louvre: Histoire et descriptions*. Paris: C. de Mourgues Frères, 1857.

La Maddalena 1986 = *La Maddalena tra sacro e profano: Da Giotto a De Chirico*, catalogue of the exhibition (Florence, Palazzo Pitti, 1986), edited by Marilena Mosco. Milan/Florence: Mondadori–La Casa Usher, 1986.

La rencontre des héros 2002 = *La rencontre des héros : Regards croisés sur les émaux peints de la Renaissance appartenant aux collections du Petit Palais, Musée des Beaux-Arts de la Ville de Paris et du Musée Municipal de l'Évêché de Limoges*, catalogue of the exhibition (Paris, Musée du Petit Palais; Limoges, Musée Municipal de l'Évêché, 2002–2004), edited by François Barbe and Veronique Notin. Limoges: Musée Municipal de l'Évêché, 2002.

Lavedan 1913 = Lavedan, Pierre. Léonard Limosin et les émailleurs français. Paris: Henri Laurens, 1913.

Lebedel 2004 = Lebedel, Hèlène. "Un Saint Jean-Baptiste d'aprés Léonard de Vinci au château de Blois." *Cahiers du château et des musées de Blois* 35 (2004): 6–21.

Le matricole degli orefici 1977 = *Le matricole degli orefici di Milano: Per la storia della Scuola di S. Eligio dal 1311 al 1773*, edited by Daniela Romagnoli. Milan: Associazione Orafa Lombarda, 1977.

Leonardo da Vinci 1883 = Leonardo da Vinci. The Literary Works of Leonardo da Vinci. Edited by Jean Paul Richter. 2 Vols. London: Sampson Low, Marston, Searle & Rivington 1883.

Leonardo da Vinci 1995 = Leonardo da Vinci. *Libro di Pittura: Codice Urbinate Lat. 1270 nella Biblioteca Apostolica Vaticana*. Edited by Carlo Pedretti, text estabilished by Carlo Vecce. Florence: Giunti, 1995.

Leonardo da Vinci 1999 = *Leonardo da Vinci: I documenti e le testimonianze contemporanee*. Edited by Edoardo Villata, preface by Pietro C. Marani. Milan: Ente Raccolta Vinciana, 1999.

Leonardo da Vinci 2011 = *Leonardo da Vinci: Painter at the Court of Milan*, catalogue of the exhibition (London, The National Gallery, 2011-2012). London: The National Gallery, 2011.

Leone de Castris 1981 = Leone de Castris, Pierluigi. "Lo smalto champlevé a Limoges." In *Medioevo e produzione artistica di serie: Smalti di Limoges e avori gotici in Campania*, catalogue of the exhibition (Naples, Museo Duca di Martina, 1981–1982), edited by Paola Giusti and Pierluigi Leone de Castris, pp. 13–32. Florence: Centro Di, 1981.

Leproux 2002 = Leproux, Guy-Michel. "Les retables de la Sainte-Chapelle commandés en 1553 à Léonard Limosin." *Commission municipale du vieux Paris: Procès-verbaux, Année 2001* (2002): 120–123.

Linas 1868 = Linas, Charles de. *L'histoire du travail à l'Exposition Universelle de 1867*. Arras-Paris: Rousseau-Leroy-Didron, 1868.

Lippmann 1888 = Lippmann, Friedrich. *The Art of Wood-Engraving in Italy in the Fifteenth Century*. London: Bernard Quaritch, 1888.

Longpérier 1842 = Longpérier, Adrien Prévost de. "Description de quelques monuments émaillés du Moyen Âge." *Le cabinet de l'amateur et de l'antiquaire: Revue des tableaux et des estampes anciennes, des objets d'art, d'antiquité et de curiosité* 1 (1842): 145–160.

Lorentz 2011 = Lorentz, Philippe. "Jen Hey et le vitrail: Une oeuvre méconnue du peintre des Bourbons à la cathédrale de Moulins." In *Peindre en France à la Renaissance*, I, *Les courants stylistiques au temps de Louis XII et de François Ier*, edited by Frédéric Elsig, 179–193. Cinisello Balsamo: Silvana, 2011.

Marani 1989 = Marani, Pietro C. *Leonardo: Catalogo completo dei dipinti*. Florence: Cantini, 1989.

Marquet de Vasselot 1912 = Marquet de Vasselot, Jean-Joseph. "L'orfèvrerie et l'émaillerie au XVe siècle." In *Histoire de l'art depuis les premiers temps chrétiens jusqu'à nos jours* 1, edited by André Michel, 448–462. Paris: A. Colin, 1912.

Marquet de Vasselot 1921 = Marquet de Vasselot, Jean-Joseph. *Les émaux limousins de la fin du XVe siècle et la première partie du XVIe: Étude sur Nardon Pénicaud et ses contemporains*, 2 vols. Paris: Auguste Picard, 1921.

McKendrick and Doyle 2007 = McKendrick, Scot, and Kathleen Doyle. *Bible Manuscripts: 1400 Years of Scribes and Scripture*. London: British Library, 2007.

Mérimée 1832 = Mérimée, Prosper. *Chronique du règne de Charles IX (1572)*. Paris: H. Fournier, 1832.

Meyer 1895 = Meyer, Alfred. *L'art de l'émail de Limoges ancien et moderne*. Paris: Alfred Meyer, 1895.

Michaels 1964–1965 = Michaels, Peter E. "Technical Observations on Early Painted Enamels of Limoges: Their Materials, Structure, Technique and Deterioration." *Journal of the Walters Art Gallery* 27–28 (1964–1965): 21–43.

Milazzo 1991 = Milazzo, Natalia. "Alcune osservazioni sull'evoluzione della tecnica dello smalto in un gruppo di opere lombarde tra la fine del XV e l'inizio del XVI secolo." *Annali della Scuola Normale Superiore di Pisa* s. III, 21, no. 1 (1991): 275–291.

Molinier 1885 = Molinier, Émile. *Dictionnaire des émailleurs depuis le Moyer Âge jusque a la fin du XVIIIe siècle*. Paris: J. Rouam, 1885.

Molinier 1891 = Molinier, Émile. L'émaillerie. Paris: Hachette, 1891.

Molinier 1903 = Molinier, Émile. *Collections du Château de Goluchów: Objets d'art du Moyen Âge et de la Renaissance*. Paris: E. Moreau, 1903.

Monroe 1977 = Monroe, William H. "Painted Renaissance Enamels from Limoges." *Bulletin of the Art Institute of Chicago* 71, no. 6 (1977): 10–13.

Musée des Thermes 1860 = *Musée des Thermes et de l'Hôtel de Cluny: Catalogue et description des objets d'art de l'antiquité du Moyen Âge et de la Renaissance exposés au musée*. Paris: Hôtel de Cluny, 1860.

Museo Poldi Pezzoli 1981 = *Museo Poldi Pezzoli: Orologi, oreficerie*. Milan: Electa, 1981.

Netzer 1999 = Netzer, Susanne. *Maleremails aus Limoges: Der Bestand des Berliner Kunstgewerbemuseums*. Berlin: G. & A., 1999.

Neue Forschungen zum Malermail aus Limoges 2004 = *Neue Forschungen zum Malermail aus Limoges / New Research on Limoges Painted Enamels*, conference proceedings (Braunschweig, 2002), edited by Irmgard Müsch and Heike Stege. Braunschweig: Herzog Anton Ulrich-Museum, 2004.

Nouvelles acquisitions 1995 = *Nouvelles acquisitions du Départment des Objects d'art 1990–1994*. Paris: Réunion des Musées Nationaux, 1995.

Oreficeria sacra italiana 1990 = *Oreficeria sacra italiana: Museo Nazionale del Bargello*, edited. by Marco Collareta and Antonella Capitanio. Florence: SPES, 1990.

Oro dai Visconti agli Sforza 2011 = *Oro dai Visconti agli Sforza: Smalti e oreficerie nel Ducato di Milano*, catalogue of the exhibition (Milan, Museo Diocesano, 2011–2012), edited by Paola Venturelli. Cinisello Balsamo: Silvana, 2011.

Panofsky 1927 = Panofsky, Erwin. "'Imago pietatis': Ein Beitrag zur Typengeschichte der 'Schmerzensmanns und der 'Maria Mediatrix.'" In *Festschrift für Max J. Friedländer zum 60. Geburtstage*, 261–308. Leipzig: H. Seeman, 1927.

Panofsky 1953 = Panofsky, Erwin. *Early Netherlandish Painting: Its Origins and Character*, 2 vols. Cambridge, Mass.: Harvard University Press, 1953.

Panofsky 1956 = Panofsky, Erwin. "Jean Hey's 'Ecce Homo': Speculation about Its Author, Its Donor, and Its Iconography." *Bulletin des Musée Royaux des Beaux-Arts* 5 (1956): 94–138.

Panofsky [1943] 1967 = Panofsky, Erwin. *The Life and Art of Albrecht Dürer*, 2 vols. Princeton: Princeton University Press, 1943.

Pedretti 1972 = Pedretti, Carlo. *Leonardo da Vinci: The Royal Palace at Romorantin*. Cambridge, Mass.: Harvard University Press, 1972.

Pedretti 2008 = Pedretti, Carlo. *Leonardo & io*. Milan: Mondadori, 2008.

Pedretti and Melani 2014 = Pedretti, Carlo, and Margherita Melani. *La Madonna dei fusi di Leonardo da Vinci: Tre versioni per la sua prima committenza francese / The Yarnwinder Madonna of Leonardo da Vinci: The Three Versions for His First French Commission*. Poggio a Caiano: CB Edizioni Grandi Opere, 2014.

Pellegrin 1969 = Pellegrin, Élisabeth. *La bibliothéque des Visconti et des Sforza ducs de Milan*. Florence: Olschki, 1969.

"Pénicaud" 1956 = "Pénicaud." In Emmanuel Bénézit, *Dictionnaire critique et documentaire des peintres, sculpteurs, dessinateurs et graveurs de tous les temps et de tous le pays par un group d'*écrivains *spécialistes français et étragers* VI, 582–583. Paris: Gründ, 1956.

Petrassi 1982 = Petrassi, Mario. *Gli smalti in Italia*. Rome: Editalia, 1982.

Popelin 1866 = Popelin, Claudius. *L'émail des Peintres*. Paris: Lévy, 1866.

Popelin 1891 = Popelin, Claudius. "Les émaux peints." In *La collection Spitzer: Antiquité, Moyen-Âge, Renaissance* 2, edited by Frédéric Spitzer, 1–72. Paris: Quantin, 1891.

Purcell 1999 = Purcell, Katherine. *Falize: A Dynasty of Jewelers*. London: Thames & Hudson, 1999.

Résumé du catalogue 1893 = *Résumé du catalogue des objets d'art et de haute curiosité antiques, du*

Moyen Âge et de la Renaissance composant l'important et précieuse collection Spitzer dont la vente publique . . . du lundi 17 au vendredi 16 juin 1893. Paris: E. Menard, 1893.

Robinson 1861 = Robinson, John Charles. *Notice of the Principal Works of Art in the Collection of Hollingworth Magniac*. London: Cundall, Dowens, 1861.

Röhrs and Stege 2004 = Röhrs, Stephan, and Heike Stege. "Analysis of Limoges Painted Enamels from the 16th to 19th Centuries by Using a Portable Micro X-Ray Fluorescence Spectrometer." *X-Ray Spectrometry* 33, no. 6 (2004): 396–401.

Ross 1941 = Ross, Marvin C. "The Master of the Orléans Triptych: Enameller and Painter." *Journal of the Walters Art Gallery* 4 (1941): 9–25.

Ross 1949 = Ross, Marvin C. "A Method for Detecting False Limoges Painted Enamels." *Journal of the Walters Art Gallery* 12 (1949): 41–53.

Rossi 1889 = Rossi, Umberto. "La collezione Carrand nel Museo Nazionale di Firenze." *Archivio storico dell'arte* 2, no. 1 (1889): 10–23, 215–228.

Rubinstein-Bloch 1926 = Rubinstein-Bloch, Stella. *Catalogue of the Collection of George and Florence Blumenthal, New York*, III, *Works of Art, Mediaeval and Renaissance*. Paris: A. Lévy, 1926.

Sammer 2009 = Sammer, Jan. "L'invitation du roi." In *Léonard de Vinci* 2009, pp. 29–33.

Schwahn 2014 = Schwahn, Birgit. "Enamel Insert Restorations on Limoges Painted Enamels: A Study on a Remarkable Nineteenth-Century Restoration Technique with Particular Attention to the Original Paillon Designs." *Studies in Conservation* 59, no. 3 (2014): 161–179.

Sciolla 1998 = Sciolla, Gianni Carlo. *Bergognone giovane: Problemi iconografici*. In *Ambrogio da Fossano detto il Bergognone: Un pittore per la Certosa*, catalogue of the exhibition (Pavia, Musei Civici e Museo della Certosa, 1998), edited by Gianni Carlo Sciolla, 139–151. Milan: Skira, 1998.

Seguin 1961 = Seguin, Jean-Pierre. "La découverte de l'Italie par les soldats de Charles VIII 1494–1495, d'après les journaux occasionnels du temps." *Gazette des Beaux-Arts* 58 (1961): 127–134.

Sframeli 2004 = Sframeli, Maria. "Smalti." In *La storia del Bargello: 100 capolavori da scoprire*, edited by Beatrice Paolozzi Strozzi, pp. 315–323. Cinisello Balsamo: Silvana, 2004.

Shell and Sironi 1989 = Shell, Janice, and Grazioso Sironi. "Documents for Copies of the 'Cenacolo' and the 'Virgin of Rocks' by Bramantino, Marco d'Oggiono, Bernardino de' Conti and Cesare Magni." *Raccolta Vinciana* 23 (1989): 103–117.

Slitine 1999 = Slitine, Florence. "A propos d'émaux de Limoges du XIXe siècle: Les reproductions de la maison Samson." *Sèvres: Revue de la Societé des Amis du Musée National de Céramique* 8 (1999): 68–80.

Slitine 2002 = Slitine, Florence. *Samson génie de l'imitation*, preface by Tamara Préaud. Paris: Charles Massin, 2002.

Smalti e gioielli 1986 = *Smalti e gioielli dal XV al XIX secolo: Museo Nazionale del Bargello*, catalogue of the exhibition (Florence, Museo Nazionale del Bargello, 1986), edited by Yvonne Hackenbroch. Florence: SPES, 1986.

Souchal 1966 = Souchal, Geneviève. "L'émail de Nardon Pénicaud, dit 'de Saint-Pierre de Royan.'" *Bullettin Monumental* 124, no. 1 (1966): 102–104.

Souchal 1975–1976 = Souchal, Geneviève. "Le mécénat de la famille d'Amboise." *Bulletin de la Société des Antiquaires de l'Ouest et des Musées de Poitiers* s. IV, 13 (1975–1976): 485–526, 567–612.

Speel 1998 = Speel, Erika. *Dictionary of Enamelling: History and Techniques*. Aldershot: Ashgate, 1998.

Speel 2008 = Speel, Erika. *Painted Enamels: An Illustrated Survey 1500–1920*. London: Lund Humphries, 2008.

Speel and Bronk 2001 = Speel, Erika, and Heike Bronk. "Enamel Painting: Materials and Recipes in Europe from c. 1500 to c. 1920." *Berliner Beiträge zur Archäometrie* 18 (2001): 43–100.

Sterling 1938 = Sterling, Charles. *La peinture française: Les primitifs*. Paris: Floury, 1938.

Supino 1898 = Supino, Igino Benvenuto. *Catalogo del R. Museo Nazionale di Firenze (Palazzo del Potestà)*. Rome: Tipografia dell'Unione Cooperativa Editrice, 1898.

Syta et al. 2018 = Syta, Olga, Luiza Kępa, Anna Mistewicz, Catia Wesołowska, and Barbara Wagner. "In Situ Study of Limoges Painted Enamels by Portable X-Ray Fluorescence Supported by Laser Ablation Inductively Coupled Plasma Mass Spectrometry Analysis of Micro-Samples." *Microchemical Journal* 137 (2018): 37–44.

Tait 1999 = Tait, Hugh. "Limoges Enamels—Some 'Signatures' and 'Dates': Problems for the Scientist?" *Berliner Beiträge zur Archäometrie* 16 (1999). 137–143.

Texier 1842 = Texier, Jacques-Rémi-Antoine. "Essai historique et descriptifs sur les argentiers et les émailleurs de Limoges." *Mémoires de la Société des Antiquaires de l'Ouest* (1842): 77–347.

Texier 1843 = Texier, Jacques-Rémi-Antoine. *Essai historique et descriptif sur les émailleurs et les argentiers de Limoges*. Poitier: Saurin Frères, 1843.

Tixier 2016 = Tixier, Frédéric. "Un certain goût pour l'orfèvrerie mosane au XIXe siècle: Quelques remarques sur la collection parisienne d'Alexandre Basilewsky." In *Orfèvrerie septentrionale, XIIe et XIIIe siècle*, conference proceedings, Trésor et Archéforum (Liège, Université de Liège, 2014), edited by Philippe George, 121–137. Liège: Trésor de la Cathédrale, 2016.

Tixier 2021 = Tixier, Frederic. "Être religieux et collectionneur d'objets médiévaux dans la seconde moitié du XIXe siècle." In *Collectionner aux XIXe et XXe siècles: Les hommes, l'esprit et les lieux*, conference proceedings (Paris, Musée de la Chasse et de la Nature, 2011), edited by Pauline Prevost-Marcilhacy and Patrick Michel, 99–108. 2021. https://www.chassenature.org/documentaires/actes-de-colloques/collectionner-aux-xixe-et-xxe-siecles.

Tonnellier 1965 = Tonnellier, Chanoine. "La véritable destination de l'émail dit 'Saint Pierre de Royan.'" *Revue du Bas-Poitu et des Provinces de l'Ouest* 76, no. 2 (1965): 105–118.

Van der Linden et al. 2010 = Van der Linden, Verner, Olivier Schalm, Jos Houbraken, Mienke Thomas, Eva Meesdom, Annemie De Vos, Rita Van Dooren, Hans Nieuwdorp, Elsje Janssen, and Koen Janssens. "Chemical Analysis of 16th to 19th Century Limoges School 'Painted Enamel' Objects in Three Museums of the Low Countries." *X-Ray Spectrometry* 39, no. 2 (2010): 112–121.

Vecce 1997 = Vecce, Carlo. "Piglia da Gian di Paris." *Achademia Leonardi Vinci* 10 (1997): 208–213.

Vecce 1998 = Vecce, Carlo. *Leonardo*. Rome: Salerno, 1998.

Vecce 2003 = Vecce, Carlo. "Léonard de Vinci et la France." In *Léonard de Vinci: Dessins et manuscrits*, catalogue of the exhibition (Paris, Musée du Louvre, 2003), edited by Françoise Viatte and Varena Forcione, 21–26. Paris: Réunion des Musées Nationaux, 2003.

Vente du cabinet 1843 = "Vente du cabinet de M. Didier Petit, de Lyon." *Le cabinet de l'amateur et de l'antiquaire: Revue des tableaux et des estampes anciennes, des objets d'art, d'antiquité et de curiosité* 2 (1843): 198–199.

Venturelli 2002 = Venturelli, Paola. *Leonardo da Vinci e le arti preziose: Milano tra XV e XVI secolo*, preface by Carlo Pedretti. Venice: Marsilio, 2002.

Venturelli 2003 = Venturelli, Paola. *Smalto, oro e preziosi: Oreficerie e arti suntuarie nel Ducato di Milano tra Visconti e Sforza*. Venice: Marsilio, 2003.

Venturelli 2008 = Venturelli, Paola. *Esmaillée à la façon de Milan: Smalti nel Ducato di Milano da Bernabò Visconti a Ludovico il Moro*. Venice: Marsilio, 2008.

Venturelli 2010 = Venturelli, Paola. *Gli smalti dipinti Limoges: Museo Diocesano Francesco Gonzaga*, preface by Véronique Notin. Mantua: Publi Paolini, 2010.

Venturelli 2012 = Ventureli, Paola. "La 'Pace del Moderno' del Museo Diocesano Francesco Gonzaga di Mantova." *OADI: Rivista dell'Osservatorio per le Arti Decorative in Italia* 6 (2012), www.unipa.it/oadi/rivista.

Venturelli 2018 = Venturelli, Paola. "Leonardo da Vinci tra mappamondi, pietre dure e cristalli milanesi (e Caradosso)." *OADI: Rivista dell'Osservatorio per le Arti Decorative in Italia* 18 (2018). www.unipa.it/oadi/rivista.

Venturelli 2020 = Venturelli, Paola. "Una sola amo con fede: Medaglie ed enseignes tra Milano e Roma, Leonardo da Vinci e Caradosso." In *Oltre l'ornamento: Il gioiello tra identità, lusso e moderazione*, conference proceedings (Padua, Sala delle Edicole, Corte dell'Arco Vallaresso, 2019), edited by Giovanna Baldassin Molli and Serena Franzon, 29–42. Palermo: Palermo University Press, 2020.

Venturelli 2021a = Venturelli, Paola. *Arte orafa milanese 1450–1527: Leonardo da Vinci tra creatività e tecnica, con un'appendice su Caradosso*. Cinisello Balsamo: Silvana, 2021.

Venturelli 2021b = Venturelli, Paola. "Milano / Leonardo da Vinci / Venezia e l'arte vetraria: Con Giovanni Agostino da Lodi e il vetro rosso." *OADI: Rivista dell'Osservatorio per le Arti Decorative in Italia* 24 (2021). www.unipa.it/oadi/rivista.

Venturelli 2022 = Venturelli, Paola. "'Lustro' e 'trasparente,' 'oro,' 'foglie,' 'rubino balasscio,' 'vetri' (con acqua e cristallo): Qualche osservazione per Leonardo e i materiali delle arti preziose." In *Leonardo da Vinci e la lingua della pittura in Europa (secoli XIV– XVII)*, conference proceedings (Paris/Turin, 2019), edited by Margherita Quaglino and Anna Sconza, 309–317. Florence: Olschki, 2022.

Venturelli forthcoming = Venturelli, Paola. "'E Leda ne' Fabbri' (Windsor, Royal Library 12281r): Leonardo and Caradosso, along with a Drawing by a Lombard Artist." *Leonardo Studies* (forthcoming).

Verdier 1967 = Verdier, Philippe. *The Walters Art Gallery Catalogue of Painted Enamels of the Renaissance*. Baltimore: Trustees of the Walters Art Gallery, 1967.

Verdier 1977 = Verdier, Philippe. *The Frick Collection: An Illustrated Catalogue*, VIII, *Enamels Rugs and Silvers: Limoges Painted Enamels, Oriental Rugs and English Silver*. New York: Frick Collection, 1977.

Verdier 1995 = Verdier, Philippe. "Limoges Enamels." In *The Taft Museum: European Decorative Arts*, 328–404. New York: Hudson Hill, 1995.

Verità et al. 2018 = Verità, Marco, Isabelle Biron, Andrea Cagnini, Simone Porcinai, and Françoise Barbe. "The So-Called Venetian Enamelled Copper Artworks of the Italian Renaissance: The Technology and Provenance of the Enamels—An Analytical Approach." *Archaeometry* 60, no. 2 (2018): 233–254. https://doi.org/10.1111/arcm.12312.

Verne [1857] 2008 = Verne, Jules. *Salon de 1857: Texte intégral* établi, *présenté et annoté par Volker Dehs*, 2008. www.jules-verne.eu/.

Villata 2013 = Villata, Edoardo. "Charles d'Amboise, commanditaire et protecteur des arts dans le duché de Milan." In *Georges Ier d'Amboise* (2103): 199–208.

Westgarth 2009 = Westgarth, Mark. *A Biographical Dictionary of Nineteenth Century Antique and Curiosity Dealers*. Glasgow: Regional Furniture Society, 2009.

Wolff 2011 = Wolff, Martha. "Le processus créative de Jean Hey." In *Peindre en France à la Renaissance*, I, *Les courants stylistiques au temps de Louis XII et de François Ier*, edited by Frédéric Elsig, 195–213. Cinisello Balsamo: Silvana, 2011.

Wypyski 2004 = Wypyski, Mark T. "Identification of 19th C. Limoges Painted Enamels at the Metropolitan Museum of Art: Characterization of Enamel Compositions." In *Neue Forschungen zum Maleremail aus Limoges* (2004): 123–131.

Zucchiatti et al. 2006 = Zucchiatti, Alessandro, Anne Bouquillon, Ildiko Katona, and Alessandra D'Alessandro. "The Della Robbia Blue: A Case Study for the Use of Cobalt Pigments in Ceramics during the Italian Reinassance." *Archaeometry* 48, no. 1 (2006): 131–152. https://doi.org/10.1111/j.1475-4754.2006.00247.

INDEX OF NAMES

PHOTO CREDITS

Alamy stock photo: fig. 1 p. 18.

Baltimore, The Walters Art Museum: fig. 6 p. 25, fig. 11 p. 28, figs. 12-13 p. 29, fig. 1 p. 39.

Brussels, Musée Royal des Beaux-Arts de Belgique, photo: J. Geleyns: fig. 8 p. 25.

Cambridge, The Fitzwilliam Museum: fig. 3 p. 51.

Florence, Ministero della Cultura - Opificio delle Pietre Dure: pp. 36-37, pp. 42-43, pp. 48-49, figs. 1-7 pp. 60-63, fig. 1 p. 65, fig. 2 p. 66, fig. 1 p. 68, figs. 2-3 p. 69; Museo Nazionale del Bargello: fig. 1 p. 12, figs. 2-3 p. 13, fig. 4 p. 14 fig. 10 p. 27.

Granada, Museo de Bellas Artes: fig. 5 p. 55.

London, © Victoria & Albert Museum: fig. 2 p. 20.

Mantua, Museo Diocesano Francesco Gonzaga: fig. 2 p. 40.

New York, The Metropolitan Museum of Art: fig. 5 p. 24, fig. 1 p. 46, fig. 2 p. 47.

Paris, Musée du Louvre: fig. 3 p. 21; Musée des Arts Décoratifs: fig. 2 p. 50.

Plainville, Winter Associates of CT: fig. 7 p. 57.

Rome, Ministero della Cultura – Galleria Borghese: fig. 9 p. 26; ICCD – Gabinetto Fotografico Nazionale – Fondo MPI: fig. 5 p. 15, fig. 6 p. 56.

Washington, Courtesy National Gallery of Art: fig. 4 p. 23.

Officina Libraria – Museo Nazionale del Bargello

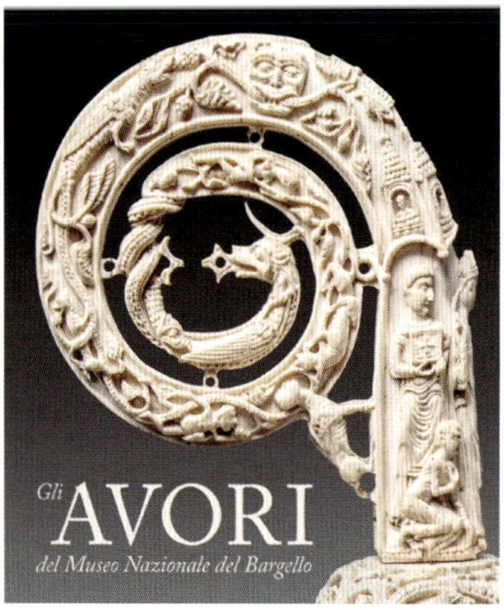

Gli Avori
del Museo Nazionale del Bargello

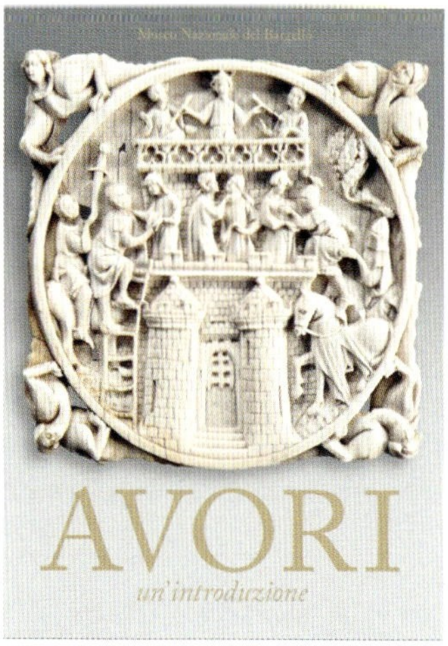

Avori. Un'introduzione

Printed on the presses of Petruzzi, Città di Castello (Perugia), Italy
in the month of July 2022

FSC
www.fsc.org
MIX
Paper from
responsible sources
FSC® C017635

ex Officina Libraria Jellinek et Gallerani